PREPARING
FOR YOUR
Endowment

OTHER BOOKS BY CORY B. JENSEN

Understanding Your Endowment

PREPARING
FOR YOUR
Endowment

CORY B. JENSEN

CFI
AN IMPRINT OF CEDAR FORT, INC.
SPRINGVILLE, UTAH

ISBN 13: 978-1-4621-1965-3

Published by CFI, an imprint of Cedar Fort, Inc.
2373 W. 700 S., Springville, UT 84663
Distributed by Cedar Fort, Inc., www.cedarfort.com

LIBRARY OF CONGRESS CATALOGING-IN-PUBLICATION DATA

Names: Jensen, Cory B., 1966- author.
Title: Preparing for your endowment / Cory B. Jensen.
Description: Springville, Utah : CFI, an imprint of Cedar Fort, Inc., [2016]
  | Includes bibliographical references and index.
Identifiers: LCCN 2016043382 (print) | LCCN 2016045171 (ebook) | ISBN
  9781462119653 (perfect bound : alk. paper) | ISBN 9781462127368 (epub,
  pdf, mobi)
Subjects: LCSH: Temple endowments (Mormon Church) | Temple work (Mormon
  Church) | Church of Jesus Christ of Latter-day Saints--Doctrines. | Mormon
  Church--Doctrines.
Classification: LCC BX8643.T4 J45 2016 (print) | LCC BX8643.T4 (ebook) | DDC
  264/.09332--dc23
LC record available at https://lccn.loc.gov/2016043382

Cover design by Kinsey Beckett
Cover design © 2017 by Cedar Fort, Inc.
Edited and typeset by Rebecca Bird

Printed in the United States of America

10 9 8 7 6 5 4 3 2 1

Printed on acid-free paper

To my children and grandchildren.

CONTENTS

CONTENTS

MENTORS INTERNATIONAL

Mentors International works to help lift the poor out of poverty. They do this by helping families—mostly women trying to support their children—receive critical business training and microcredit loans to start or grow small business ventures. Mentors International provides a hand-up rather than a handout.

As the loans are repaid, the funds are then redeployed to help other families in need. In this way, donations to Mentors become perpetual gifts. Over the past twenty-five years, Mentors has helped lift over 3.5 million individuals out of poverty and onto the path to prosperity. The stories of these individuals are inspiring. Many started with nothing and are now sending their children to college and employing others in their communities.

For further information, or to make a donation, visit www.mentors international.org. All of the author's proceeds from this book are being donated to Mentors and other similar charitable organizations founded to serve those in need around the world.

PREFACE

In preparing to attend the temple for their own ordinances, LDS Church members and leaders often spend a lot of time and effort focused on personal worthiness. Though important, worthiness is only one part of the needed preparation. President Ezra Taft Benson stated, "I believe a proper understanding or background will immeasurably help prepare our youth for the temple."[1] Too many members show up to the temple, worthy to be there, but unprepared to comprehend the meaning of the temple ordinances. As a result, many leave the temple two hours later wondering what just happened.

Sometimes in the excitement and focus of major life events like missions and marriage, the temple experience becomes secondary—merely a prerequisite to the seemingly more important things. This attitude further compounds the problem. For example, some young adults may be so caught up in mission or wedding plans that they give little thought to preparing for and receiving their own endowment. Being unprepared, they may fail to grasp its significance in their lives.

Your personal temple endowment can and should be a deeply meaningful experience. It is an important life event in and of itself. Baptism begins our journey as Christ's disciples. It symbolizes a spiritual rebirth. We spend a lot of time and emphasis in preparing for it. After our baptism and confirmation (and not counting the sacrament), the next gospel ordinances that we receive for ourselves are in the temple. The initiatory ordinances of the temple are a symbolic completion of the spiritual rebirth started by our baptism. You are given additional blessings and promises from the Lord. Following this initiation into His house, the endowment ceremony then outlines the path to spiritual maturity and power. As such, these ordinances mark a serious transition in our journey as disciples. The outpouring of the spirit we receive in the temple helps to sanctify and strengthen us in that journey.

In Book of Mormon times, the Nephites kept the law of Moses along with its associated ordinances in their temples (see 2 Nephi 5:10). Interestingly enough, we find among them two responses to these things. Many of the Nephites were taught the law of Moses and what it meant (see Jarom 1:11). They observed the ceremonies but also understood the underlying purpose, which was to point them to the Messiah. On the other hand, others among the Nephites made the law of Moses an end in itself. This group participated in the same ceremonies, but they failed to grasp the meaning, believing instead that the rituals alone saved them.

Sherem, the anti-Christ, provides an example of the second group when he accused Jacob of perverting the law of Moses into the worship of a being that would come in the future (see Jacob 7:7). Ironically, that was precisely the intended purpose of the law of Moses: it was meant to bring the people unto Christ. And yet, Sherem completely missed the point. Likewise, the wicked priests of Noah taught that salvation came by the law of Moses rather than through Christ (see Mosiah 12:31–32). They believed it was their sacrifices and the rituals that brought about salvation. Both groups (the righteous Nephites and the wicked priests) participated in the same ordinances of the law of Moses, but one group saw through the symbols and understood what they really meant and the other group did not.

We risk the same problem in approaching our temple and its ordinances. Our temple ordinances are similarly about Christ and coming unto Him. We all need to be taught, not only the ordinances, but also their underlying meanings. Parents must help their children gain understanding—otherwise they may simply end up going through the motions without any real comprehension. Many parents recognize this but find it to be a daunting challenge. President Benson said, "Because of its sacredness we are sometimes reluctant to say anything about the temple to our children and grandchildren. As a consequence . . . when they go there, they do so without much background to prepare them for the obligations and covenants they enter into."[2]

PREFACE

The intent of this book is to help Church members prepare for their own temple endowment. This book has primarily been written for the young men and young women who are making these preparations. It is my hope that if you are preparing for your own temple experience that you will involve your parents or a trusted friend who is endowed in your preparation. Read this book together and discuss it with them. Ask them questions. Talk things through so that when you go to the temple for the first time, it will be a deeply meaningful experience in your life. Together, you may want to use the chapters in this book as a series of personal temple preparation lessons.

The temple truly has been one of the greatest blessings of my life. I pray it will be the same for you. If you are not yet endowed, do whatever you need to do in your life to be worthy and prepared to enter. The blessings awaiting you there are worth the effort to obtain them. The temple testifies of our Savior and our relationship with Him. Ultimately, it is meant to bring us unto Him.

My first book, *Understanding Your Endowment*, was meant for Church members who were already endowed and familiar with the temple ceremonies. At the time of its publication, I had not planned to write another book. I have tried to minimize any overlap between the two and would recommend you read both; but please, read this one first. If I could go back and write them over, I would probably arrange some content differently between the two volumes. There are some topics that are explained more fully in *Understanding Your Endowment*. As a result, this work will refer you to that one in several places for additional details or more information.

I alone am responsible for the content of this volume. Though it reflects my beliefs, it does not in any way represent official doctrine of The Church of Jesus Christ of Latter-day Saints. When it comes to the temple, I am still very much a student and don't consider myself qualified as a teacher. Take what seems helpful to you from this and discard anything that does not. It is my hope and prayer that you will find it useful in preparing for and coming to understand your personal endowment.

Finally, I wish to acknowledge and express heartfelt thanks to the following individuals for their contributions to this book: Traci Jensen, Jessica Flory, Dedra Tregaskis, Sherrie Gavin, Mark Shields, Kristina Murri, David Burbidge, Craig Jenkins, Don Coplin, Matthew Kennedy, Joel Jenkins, and the helpful staff at Cedar Fort.

Part 1
YOUR FOUNDATION

INTRODUCTION

*P*roper temple preparation begins long before the day you enter the temple's sacred grounds. It begins even before you sit down with your bishop and stake president for worthiness interviews. In part 1, we will discuss the foundation you need before entering the temple to receive your endowment. That foundation begins with your testimony, which should be centered on Christ and His gospel, the central part of which is the Atonement and the doctrine of Christ. We will explore this doctrine in greater detail and consider how it relates to the temple.

Before we begin, pause for a moment to reflect on another question: why do you want to go to the temple? Elder Boyd K. Packer taught, "Curiosity is not a preparation. Deep interest itself is not a preparation. Preparation for the ordinances includes preliminary steps: faith, repentance, baptism, confirmation, worthiness, a maturity and dignity worthy of one who comes invited as a guest into the house of the Lord."[3] We will consider these steps of faith, repentance, and baptism, as outlined by Elder Packer, in this section. Though these may seem to be elementary, please don't skip over them. They are worth more careful thought and consideration than we sometimes give them. We will examine them in greater detail.

If curiosity and deep interest are not sufficient, why then should you be endowed? If you have gained a testimony of your own, and if you have entered into and are following the path outlined by the doctrine of Christ, and if you are seeking to come unto Him, then the temple will be a great blessing in your life. If not, then you likely won't receive much benefit from it.

As part of your endowment, you will receive promises and blessings from the Lord. You will be taught more of His ways and may feel of His Spirit and love in rich abundance. You will make sacred covenants that can draw you closer to Him. Ultimately, your endowment is not simply about receiving additional gospel ordinances, but is to be a gift of power from heaven. The Lord explained that we may go forth from His house armed with His power, with His name upon us, His glory round about us, and His angels watching over us (see D&C 109:22).

In summary, the temple deepens our discipleship and helps bring the power of godliness into our lives (see D&C 84:20). Temple blessings are worth the price required to receive them. Prepare for them carefully. Go to the Lord's house and receive them in faith, recognizing that the ordinances witness of His great love for you and the divine destiny He has in mind for you. Enjoy the Spirit and the love you will feel there. Return to the temple often and work toward fully understanding and receiving these blessings in your daily life.

Chapter 1

YOUR TESTIMONY

As we journey through life, each of us experiences defining moments. What we choose to do with these moments often has an enormous impact on our future and on the future of others as well. Your temple endowment can and should be one of these defining moments in your life. Prior to it, you need a strong testimony, a proper foundation, and some temple preparation.

Think about your own testimony for a minute. How strong is it? How did you gain it? What could you do to strengthen it? Have you recorded or shared it recently? Are there specific experiences or moments that helped to shape it?

The entire Restoration began with such a defining moment. Have you ever wondered about Joseph Smith's experience and how it might relate to your own life? If you are not already familiar with the history of Joseph Smith found in the Pearl of Great Price, please find some time to read it and ponder its message. We are going to review parts of it together in the pages that follow and look at how his experience can apply to you as well. Perhaps this may seem like a funny place to start a book about preparing for the temple, but our individual journey to the temple actually begins with our own testimony. Joseph's life is a good example of the steps we each must follow to gain one.

JOSEPH'S STORY

Joseph Smith's story began with his birth on December 23, 1805, in Sharon, Vermont (see Joseph Smith—History 1:3). Consider the time and circumstances into which Joseph was born and grew up. How did they shape his life? Even the date of his birth seems to be significant. Every year between December 21 and 23 we experience the winter solstice in the northern hemisphere. This date marks the longest night and the shortest day of the year. It is the darkest day of the entire year. The very next day, daylight once again begins to increase. Months later, the calendar reaches the spring equinox where the night and day are equal and in balance. As weeks pass, the light continues to increase, in its gradual triumph over the darkness, until June when the summer solstice marks the longest day of the year and the shortest night. Joseph Smith's birth occurred at a time of the year with the greatest darkness but with the promise of brighter days and increased light ahead. Was that purely coincidence? Or carefully planned by God?

Other circumstances of his early life seem important as well. Only twenty-two years had passed since the end of the Revolutionary War, which had secured freedom in the new United States. These freedoms were crucial to the Restoration. Many earlier events had also contributed to the religious fervor and excitement that Joseph describes in his history at the time he was a teenager. These circumstances led Joseph to ponder some serious questions: Which church should I join? Where can I look for salvation?

You will also face many questions in your life. The years from age fourteen to twenty-four are sometimes called the *decade of decisions*. It is a time when so many of life's questions must be answered for yourself: Does God really care about me? Is the Book of Mormon true? Should I serve a mission? Who should I marry? What career is right for me? What does God want me to do with my life? These kinds of questions often require greater wisdom than we have on our own. How can we find answers?

Like Joseph, the circumstances of your life and the timing of your birth are no accident. God has purpose in these things, and He has a plan for you. Your task is to find it and to seek His help to bring it about. Let's look further at how Joseph approached the question he faced.

From his record we know that he spent a lot of time pondering on his own question. He worked to resolve it by attending the meetings of the various churches to try to figure out which was right. And he turned to the scriptures for answers. His daily life at that time must have been filled with long hours of work. There were chores to do—cows to milk, chickens to feed, land to clear, planting and harvesting, and numerous other tasks. He must have been tired at the end of each long day. Despite this, he spent some of his free time searching the Bible.

You probably have a busy schedule as well, filled with school, work, and other activities in addition to the distractions of our modern world. Joseph never had a cell phone, television, video games, or the many other things that can occupy our time. These things can have a place in our lives, but if we aren't careful, they may crowd out more important things. You've probably been told many times that you need to pray and study the scriptures. It seems to be kind of a routine answer in the Church, but it is really true. Like Joseph, we all need to spend some time searching and pondering the scriptures.[4] Many times God will answer our prayers through the scriptures. Joseph testified that it was while he was reading the scriptures that an initial answer came to him:

> I was one day reading the Epistle of James, first chapter and fifth verse, which reads: *If any of you lack wisdom, let him ask of God, that giveth to all men liberally, and upbraideth not; and it shall be given him.*
>
> Never did any passage of scripture come with more power to the heart of man than this did at this time to mine. It seemed to enter with great force into every feeling of my heart. I reflected on it again and again, knowing that if any person needed wisdom from God, I did; for how to act I did not know, and unless I could get more wisdom than I then had, I would never know. (Joseph Smith—History 1:11–12)

Stop and think about this scripture's promise for a minute. Let's rephrase it: If you need answers in your life, ask God. He gives to everyone generously and doesn't scold or find fault with you for asking. Answers will be given. That's a pretty amazing promise. And it doesn't just apply to Joseph Smith; *you* are included in that promise. You can take your questions to God for answers. If Joseph's life testifies of anything, it testifies to this truth: God will answer your sincere questions. He wants to talk with you. Your testimony needs to be based on your own experiences with the Lord.

Maybe you feel too small and unimportant. Or perhaps you are struggling with something in your life and just don't feel worthy. You might think *why would God ever want to answer me?* While those kinds of thoughts and feelings may be very real, they don't come from God. Remember that He spoke with Laman and Lemuel, Alma the younger, and the sons of Mosiah while they were sinning (see 1 Nephi 16:39, Mosiah 27:25). He also spoke with Cain (see Genesis 4:9–13). Whatever sins you may be struggling with in your life, they aren't as great as Cain's. God can still answer your prayers, even if you don't feel worthy. He often sends answers when they are most needed, not necessarily at the time we are most worthy of them.

Remember the Savior's parable of the prodigal son. Here was a kid who had wasted his inheritance and sinned deeply against his father. He probably hadn't even been grateful for what he had received until it was lost and he began to suffer the consequences of his choices. And yet notice three important things that happened. First, he ended up in the pig slop. That is always where sin leads, so to speak. No matter how fun it may seem, eventually, the lights and music stop, the party ends, and reality sets in. The nature of sin is always to leave you in the gutter of life (see Alma 30:60). It cannot be otherwise. Though Satan tries to make sin seem exciting, it will always leave you empty rather than filling you up. The good news is that at this point, the second thing happened: the young man "came to himself" (Luke 15:17). In other words, he finally realized that his life wasn't in the right place. He remembered that there was something better available to him, and so he decided to make the long journey home regardless of the cost (Luke 15:18–19). He no longer felt worthy to be called a son, but decided it was better to be a servant to his father than to serve a stranger in a far country.

The third thing occurred as he journeyed home. The scripture records that while he was still a long way from home, his father saw him and ran to greet him (see Luke 15:20). In all this time, his father had never, ever stopped loving him. He was waiting and watching for his son to return. He knew and understood the mistakes his son had made and the painful lessons he had learned. And he wanted only for him to return. And so he watched and waited, day after day. Imagine this father's joy when he finally saw his son coming home. He dropped whatever he had been working on and ran to meet his son. Likewise, no matter what mistakes you may have made in your life, please know that you have a Heavenly Father who watches and waits for your return. And as you start to repent and make the journey toward home, He, too, will run to greet you. He will answer your prayers. God has never, ever stopped loving you. He waits to speak with you.

Like the young prodigal, Joseph's life reached a similar point where he also concluded that he needed God's help. "At length I came to the conclusion that I must either remain in darkness and confusion, or else I must do as James directs, that is, ask of God. I at length came to the determination to 'ask of God'" (Joseph Smith—History 1:13). Joseph had been pondering his question for some time. He had searched the scriptures for an answer. Now he was determined to ask God.

If you are not having spiritual experiences in your life, if you are not *hearing* and *feeling* the words of the Lord to you, then it is probably because you are not following this basic pattern of searching, pondering, praying, and listening that we see here in Joseph's example. If that is the case, you can change it. Almost always, God will patiently wait until we are ready to come to Him (see D&C 88:63). However, it is usually better to seek Him on our own rather than waiting for the circumstances of our life to humble us enough to search for Him in pain and desperation.

Once Joseph decided to ask the Lord, he entered the grove and there encountered two opposing influences. Satan stepped in and tried to interfere. And his power was very real. Joseph testified that it felt as though he would be destroyed (see Joseph Smith—History 1:15–16). But exerting all his strength to call upon God, Joseph was delivered. Immediately the darkness was gone, replaced by the light! God is always stronger. The light will always triumph over darkness in the end. In His wisdom, however, God allows us to experience both. Think for a minute about some of the ways that you might experience both influences in your life. For example, you may experience a lot of adversity right before receiving your temple endowment.

Sometimes the order is reversed. We might experience a moment of spiritual clarity. Light, love, and truth flood our souls, and we feel as though we can conquer the world or overcome any challenge. We may truly feel of God's love and concern for us, and His will becomes clear. Eventually, however, the light fades and the adversary steps in, whispering doubts and questions. We may even come to wonder if the earlier experience really happened. *Was it all real? Or did I just imagine it?* It has to be that way. There must be opposition in all things (see 2 Nephi 2:11). Our faith must be tried. And, at times, we must make choices.

Each of us will often stand at crossroads in life. Before us may lie the road of discipleship and an alternative route or routes. We may pause and try to look down each as far as we can. The path that God calls us to take might seem more difficult. Other roads might seem easier by comparison, especially in the short term. But we must choose. We must pick up our little bundle of faith and doubt, courage and fear, hope and discouragement, and choose our path. Will we take the road our Savior would have us take? Do we trust Him enough to know He wants what is best for us in the long run? Or do we listen to the voices of distraction that lure us away with the promise of an easier journey? That is a very real battle, one we fight many times in our lives.

Sometimes the answers and confirmation we seek don't come until after we make our choice and begin traveling down one of the roads. Sometimes the Lord requires that we take a few steps in the dark before the light appears to illuminate the path. Until we move forward nothing can happen. You should ask yourself what would have happened if Joseph hadn't entered the Sacred Grove on that spring morning? How different would his life have been? How different would yours be today?

Joseph's experience in the grove with both influences was sudden and dramatic. Those kinds of big spiritual experiences do occur, but your own will probably start much more simply and subtly. However, if you will pay attention you can still recognize both influences in your life. You, too, can have moments when you are filled with God's love, peace, and spirit. There will also be times when Satan will try to fill you with doubt, discouragement, and fear. When those times come, follow Joseph's example: press forward calling upon God, with all your strength, until you once again emerge into the light.

In later chapters, we will discuss some ways God may answer your prayers, how to better recognize the voice of the Spirit, and why sometimes we may not get an answer. But for now, take a moment to reflect on your own life. How strong is your testimony? When was the last time you felt the Spirit in your life? When did God last speak to you? Have you ever heard His voice? What questions do you have that you would like Him to answer? What can you do to seek those answers?

PLANT THE SEED

You might be reading this and wondering if you really have a testimony. Perhaps you have one but would like it to be stronger. Maybe it has been a while since you last felt the Spirit or received an answer to your prayers. If that is the case, let this be the moment when you begin to want something more (see Enos 1:4). This is where the journey back to God begins—with a desire for something more than we have right now. You can gain a testimony by following the same steps Joseph took.

Alma compares this process to planting a seed in our hearts and letting it grow (see Alma 32:28–43). He outlines the way that we can begin to discern truth and gain a testimony. It starts very small. We first have to accept the seed (the word of God) and give it a chance to grow. That is always a choice. Once planted, the seed begins to grow, and we *feel* that it is good. This result strengthens our faith, but our knowledge still isn't perfect. It requires time, patience, care, nurturing, and more faith as the seed sprouts and the young tree grows. Alma promises that *if* we press on diligently, then eventually we receive fruit from the tree of life. A harvest eventually follows the planting.

The Savior gave a related parable about the soil (our heart) where the seed gets planted (see Matthew 13:3–9). A sower scattered seeds around a field. All of the seeds were good, but the ground where they fell was very different. Some of the seeds landed in stony places where the earth was shallow. Although these seeds sprouted and began to grow, they wilted and died in the heat of the sun. These are fair-weather disciples. When things get tough, they leave. The gospel doesn't take deep root in their lives. Other seeds landed by the side of the road and never had a chance to sprout. The birds ate them before they could begin to grow. This represents people who don't take the time or effort to understand the gospel and so it can't take root in their lives.

Still other seeds started out in good ground and began to grow, but then thorns and weeds overtook them. The small, young plants were overrun. These are people who accept the gospel but then allow the cares of daily life to push out more spiritual things. We need to be careful that hobbies, sports, friends, movies, video games, school, and other activities don't crowd out our spiritual lives.

Last of all, some seeds landed in good ground, sprouted, grew, and eventually produced fruit. It required good ground, water, sunshine, nurture, care, and time. The good news is that we can decide what kind of ground our hearts will be. The gospel seeds are good, but it is up to us to plant and then patiently nurture them as they grow. Sometimes we want the fruit without the work, but that's not the process. It takes some effort on our part, but the end harvest is totally worth it!

Alma testified that there is nothing better. "If ye will nourish the word, yea, nourish the tree as it beginneth to grow, by your faith with great diligence, and with patience, looking forward to the fruit thereof, it shall take root; and behold it shall be a tree springing up unto everlasting life. . . . By and by ye shall pluck the fruit thereof, which is most precious, which is sweet above all that is sweet, and which is white above all that is white, yea, and pure above all that is pure; and ye shall feast upon this fruit even until ye are filled, that ye hunger not, neither shall ye thirst" (Alma 32:41–42). The fruit of the tree of life is infinitely better than anything else life can offer. Nothing else fills our souls or heals us in the way that God's love can.

TWO SHELVES

Before we close this chapter, let's discuss one more thing related to our testimonies. What should we do when we run into something that just doesn't make any sense or even seems contradictory to our prior understanding?

When learning any subject, including the gospel, we first need to master the basics before tackling more advanced studies. Our understanding grows line upon line. If the gospel were math, we would work up through basic math, then algebra, geometry, and trigonometry before attempting to tackle calculus. Christ's gospel likewise contains both milk and meat. If we compared the scriptures to a math textbook, they have everything from basic math through advanced calculus. If a math textbook were written that way, it would be really confusing.

The scriptures deal with this challenge in part by using symbolism to conceal and reveal truths depending upon our preparation to see them. The basics are plain and simple, while advanced concepts are more obscure. One blessing of this is that we can continue learning from the scriptures throughout our entire lives. Keep this in mind as you study them and encounter things that you don't understand. Even chapters that we think we understand probably still contain more. For example, a few years ago I could have explained everything I knew about the first chapter of the Book of Mormon in five minutes. Today it would take much longer. There is so much more in that chapter than I used to be able to see. The Lord gives us more as we grow and are ready to receive more.

When it comes to gospel studies via the Internet, the safeguards built into scripture through symbolism are missing. Many members encounter information on the Internet related to Church history or parts of the gospel that they can't understand, and this sometimes causes serious questions or doubts to form in their minds. Some throw away their entire testimony as a result. That is a tragedy. Remember, Alma warned us that it would be a long time before we would have full knowledge. We may feel that the seed is good, but we still walk by faith without perfect knowledge. There will be many questions along the way.

What should we do when we encounter such information? How do we cope with the dissonance it can create? Some people find it helpful to create two mental shelves. On one shelf, place the things that you know. Keep and remember the sacred experiences that you receive from God. Keep your testimony there too. In fact, you may find it helpful to have a separate spiritual journal in order recall these experiences.

On the other shelf, place your questions and the things you don't yet understand. Leave them there until you find answers. If you are spiritually at the "algebra" level and yet ask "calculus" questions, it may be years before you are prepared with an adequate background to finally understand the answer. Leave it on the question shelf until the answer comes. Don't let these questions cause you to doubt or discard the things you already know, yet don't ignore them either. Keep seeking patiently for answers. If we are learning and growing, there will always be things on our shelf of unanswered questions. In fact, often as one question is answered, another one or more will take its place. This is an important part of our progress.

Let me illustrate with a personal example. Years ago, while serving as a missionary, my mission president invited all of us to read the Joseph Smith story in the Pearl of Great Price once a week for eight weeks. One evening, about the sixth or seventh week into this challenge, I sat reading Joseph's story once again. As I reached the part describing the First Vision, the spirit testified to my soul in a very powerful and personal way that Joseph really had experienced what he claimed. It was true. Regardless of what anyone else may say or print about Joseph Smith, I had received my own witness from God that he was a prophet. I have kept and treasured that witness all of my life. It belongs on the first shelf.

Some time after my mission, I learned that Joseph Smith actually gave several different accounts of his First Vision. And each account differs from the others, sometimes in significant ways. Some people use this fact (and it is true) to try to discredit Joseph. He must have made it up, they reason. He couldn't even get his story straight each time. And that is one possible explanation for why there are at least five different accounts. But because of my earlier witness from the Spirit, I rejected this idea. I wasn't sure why Joseph might have given different versions of his experience, but I knew it wasn't because he was making everything up. There must be another answer. And so this is a great example of the kind of question I could put on the second shelf. Why would Joseph leave different accounts of his First Vision?

Some time later, I noticed something that had never caught my attention before. After relating God's answer about which church to join, Joseph recorded: "many other things did he say unto me" (Joseph Smith—History 1:20). Hmmm. That got me thinking—maybe there was a lot more to the entire experience than Joseph ever related to anyone? I think that is true. I don't believe that Joseph ever detailed a completely full account of everything that occurred in the First Vision experience. He told bits and pieces at different times, to different audiences, and probably for different purposes.

It also seems reasonable that his own understanding of the significance and meaning of his experience grew over time. When he returned home, he told his mother that he had learned for himself that Presbyterianism wasn't true (see Joseph Smith—History 1:20). He seems to initially understand the vision as it related to himself. It may have been years later, before he realized what his experience also meant to the larger world. His perspective and understanding of the experience probably matured over time as he grew.

I received my patriarchal blessing at age fifteen. That was thirty-five years ago. Today, it is still the same blessing with the same words on the same paper, but I understand it much differently now than I did when I was fifteen. This seems to me to be a very reasonable explanation for why there are different accounts of the First Vision. And it is consistent with my earlier experience of the Spirit's witness that it really did occur.

This is just one example of many such questions. The point is to not discard what you have already received from the Spirit because of things that you don't yet understand. It is good to have questions. That is a crucial part of how we learn and grow. And our prior understanding may need to expand or adapt as we gain further knowledge. Be patient with the process. It can be a great blessing, if we don't throw the baby out with the bathwater, so to speak. Eventually, God can provide answers to all your questions, though some may not fully come in this life. In the meantime, walk forward with faith and confidence.

There are many critics of Joseph Smith, the Book of Mormon, the Book of Abraham, Church history, and so on. Some are seeking to disprove, discredit, and tear down the LDS beliefs. Others are simply raising honest questions that they have been unable to answer. On the flip side of the coin are apologists who are striving to defend the faith. They are trying to provide proofs of the divinity of Joseph Smith's calling, his work, and the Church today.

To me, the problem with Mormon apologetics is that it has evolved into a sort of never-ending tennis match. Both the critics and the defenders of Mormonism raise valid arguments and points to consider. Each side in turn claims victory, but eventually new arguments are put forth and new evidences are presented and the game resumes. Personally, I don't believe anyone will ever conclusively prove or disprove the First Vision, the Book of Mormon, or even something as foundational as the existence of God by these types of arguments. There will always be reasons to believe and other reasons to disbelieve. This seems to be by divine design and intent. Religion is deeply personal and subjective. One purpose behind that is to give us an opportunity to develop faith. Faith requires that we make a choice. We can choose to believe or to disbelieve. Choosing belief, according to Alma, plants the seed and begins the process.

Did the First Vision really occur? The only way to know is to receive our own witness from God. This provides us with *proof* but is not something that can be used to conclusively convince another. However, as Joseph learned, anyone who lacks wisdom can obtain it from God (see James 1:5–6). God can and does give proof if we are humble enough to seek it and willing to accept what He provides when it comes.

The *proof* is our own individual answers, experiences, or witness from God in response to our sincere asking, seeking, and knocking. The answers we receive may start very small, like the seed just beginning to sprout, but if we don't reject them, they will grow brighter and brighter until faith at last is replaced by perfect knowledge. I know the First Vision occurred because of the witness I received from God through the Spirit on that topic while serving as a missionary. That knowledge isn't something that I can give to you, but it is real enough to me that no argument that someone puts forth to the contrary will ever convince me otherwise. I have a similar witness of the Book of Mormon, the doctrine of Christ, and the temple. If you have not received your own personal witness of these things, you need to ask and seek for it until the Lord blesses you to know also.

You will have defining moments in your life. Your temple endowment should be one. Don't forget these spiritual experiences or the answers you receive from the Lord. Eventually the feelings may fade, but please don't doubt the answer you received. Rather, treasure these moments, remember them, and walk forward in faith. The Lord will help you and bless you. Before you go to the temple for your endowment, you should already have a strong foundational testimony of Christ and His gospel. If you don't, follow the steps that Joseph took to gain his.

HOMEWORK

1. What could you do to strengthen your testimony? If you don't really have a testimony, then the temple won't be of much value to you. It is not the place to go obtain one. You should have a testimony first.
2. Do you regularly study the scriptures and spend time in prayer? If not, make time and put a plan in place to regularly feed and strengthen your spirit and to draw closer to the Lord. Your connection with Him matters more than anything else.
3. Read the rest of Joseph Smith's history as contained in the Pearl of Great Price. What other lessons do you see from his life that could apply to yours?

Chapter 2
THE PLAN OF SALVATION

*O*ne of the important things that the temple teaches is the plan of salvation. Your endowment can help you discover your part in that divine plan and how it can unfold in your life. Over the next few pages, let's examine the plan of salvation from a slightly different angle—one that you will encounter in the temple.

THE ENDOWMENT VERSION

You are probably very familiar with the way the plan of salvation is generally diagrammed, as shown below.

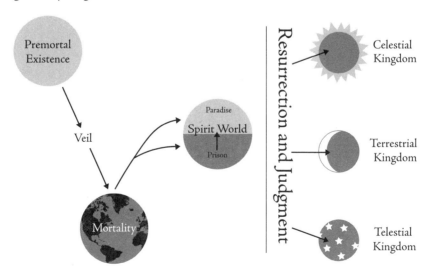

In the temple presentation, the plan of salvation centers on the tree of knowledge and the tree of life. We descended here into mortality to partake of the tree of knowledge and gain experience for ourselves. Having done so, our task is then to find our way back to the tree of life. It is the story of being cast out from God's presence and then being redeemed, or brought back into His presence once again.

In the book *The Temple Pattern*, author Marcus Ladd points out that if we really simplify the plan of salvation down to the core essence, we could diagram it this way:[5]

With Our Heavenly Father	A
Birth, Fall, and Spiritual Death	B
Mortality	C
Physical Death and Resurrection	B'
Return to Our Heavenly Father	A'

On the surface, this may look different from the first drawing of the plan of salvation, but upon closer inspection, we find that the elements are the same, just presented differently. In the pre-mortal realm, we lived with our Heavenly Parents. Because of the Fall of Adam and Eve, we have been separated from them. A veil covers our memory of the premortal existence and we walk by faith through mortality. Eventually, through death and the resurrection, we will return to the eternal realms and be reunited once again. Mortality is the crux of the matter around which everything else revolves.

Reducing the plan of salvation this way forms a chiasmus. Chiasmus is a literary form often found in ancient scripture.[6] The elements of the chiastic structure are repeated in reverse order and serve to emphasize a central, key idea. For example, we started out with our Heavenly Father and end back with our Heavenly Father (see A–A'), we die spiritually and then physically (see B–B'), and so on. The key or central element is mortality (C), separating the eternity that came before and the eternity to follow. Mortality is the focal point. It is the culmination of the preparation of the eternity that preceded it and will also determine the eternity to follow. This structure emphasizes the critical nature of mortality.

One of the added insights that the temple provides to the plan of salvation is that our *mortality* phase can actually progress through three stages. If we expand this portion of our basic diagram it could look like this:

CHAPTER 2

With Our Heavenly Father
　　Birth (Fall and Spiritual Death)
　　　　Telestial > Terrestrial > Celestial
　　Physical Death and Resurrection
Return to Our Heavenly Father

We generally think of telestial, terrestrial, and celestial as being kingdoms in heaven after the resurrection (see D&C 76). However, the endowment teaches that they are also stages here in mortality. Which one we
attain depends upon the law we choose to live (see D&C 88:22–31).

Because of the Fall, we find ourselves living in a telestial world. We
all grow up in that environment and are influenced by it. Each of us also
experiences our own individual fall as we sin. Physically and spiritually we
are separated from God. The telestial is the realm of the *natural* man and
woman (see Mosiah 3:19). It is where we all start. As part of our mortal
experience here, we are also given weakness from God as a gift to help us
learn and grow (see Ether 12:27). Because of these facts, it is inevitable
that we find ourselves stumbling and struggling. Some people live their
entire life in a telestial state, never rising above it. Others attain to and
live a terrestrial law, and a few are living celestial lives right here and now.
It depends upon the law that we obtain and choose to live by (see D&C
88:22–23).

Although we may not experience the full glory of any of these kingdoms at present, we can begin to live the laws of these kingdoms here. If
you pay attention, the endowment contains important teachings regarding these laws and the divisions between the kingdoms. The great task of
mortality is to put off the natural man or natural woman and become a
Saint through the Atonement. Or, in other words, become terrestrial and
eventually celestial persons. Once we understand that concept, the question "how do we do it?" naturally arises.

At the very heart of the plan of salvation is the Atonement. It is a
crucial part of Christ's gift to us. We are never going to rise above this
telestial world without Him. He alone is mighty to save (see Alma 34:18)!
Moving out of a telestial state requires a spiritual rebirth. We must be born
of God, changed from our carnal and fallen state to a state of righteousness
(see Mosiah 27:25). The Book of Mormon plainly teaches, "all mankind,
yea, men and women, all nations, kindreds, tongues and people, must be
born again; yea, born of God, changed from their carnal and fallen state,

to a state of righteousness, *being redeemed of God*, becoming his sons and daughters" (Mosiah 27:25; emphasis added). This is the challenge of mortality, and it does not happen without God. You were not born physically without a mother. You will not be born spiritually without God. In fact, it requires far greater effort from your mother and from God to give that birth, than it requires from you to be born. Being redeemed of God is the opposite of spiritual death. It is a return to God's presence (see Ether 3:13).

Our part in being born again is called the doctrine of Christ. This doctrine is our foundation. It is what we should build upon and return to over and over again. It is clearly outlined in the Book of Mormon by the Father and the Son. We will look at it more carefully, but before we do, I want to add a word of caution. We all want to think of ourselves as celestial material, yet the truth is that many of us are actually living telestial lives at the moment. We all start out there by default and it requires great effort on our part to rise above the telestial to attain a terrestrial and then a celestial level. Regardless of this truth, please don't let the idea or concept discourage you. Rising above the telestial is the very challenge we came down here to face. This is the journey from a natural man or woman to a saint who is spotless, sanctified, and no longer desires sin (see Alma 13:12).

Whatever successes or struggles you may have, or wherever you might currently be at on the path, the critical thing is the direction you are facing. We need to turn to the Lord. If you are not facing Him, you can always change that! The first step in our journey is recognizing where we really are and then turning to God. With that idea in mind, we should seek to assist and encourage others on their journeys as well. That requires us to love those around us. We aren't qualified to judge where another person may be at or where they are headed. A person at the bottom of a ladder heading up is far better off than a person at the top heading down. In our baptismal covenant, we aren't asked to judge, but simply to help bear one another's burdens.

THE DOCTRINE OF CHRIST

What exactly is the doctrine of Christ? Joseph Smith summarized it in the Articles of Faith: "We believe that the first principles and ordinances of the Gospel are: first, Faith in the Lord Jesus Christ; second, Repentance; third, Baptism by immersion for the remission of sins; fourth, Laying on of hands for the gift of the Holy Ghost" (Articles of Faith 1:4). This raises a question: how are these principles and ordinances *first*? Does it mean they are the first items in a long checklist of gospel requirements? Or are they first in the sense of being the most important or the basics to which we return over and over again?

When we learn to play a musical instrument, compete in a sport, or pursue any other worthwhile endeavor, there are certain basic techniques that must be mastered. For example, in basketball, the skills involved in learning to dribble, pass, and shoot the ball are practiced repeatedly. Even professional players who have learned slam dunks and other advanced moves will still continue to work on the basics. It is the same in the gospel.

These first gospel principles are clearly outlined three times in the Book of Mormon.[7] Nephi calls these first principles the doctrine of Christ (see 2 Nephi 31:2). He learned them directly from the Father and the Son (2 Nephi 31:11–15). We see very few instances in scripture where we have the words of the Father. That should be an indication to us of their importance.[8]

In the temple, God explains the purpose of life using the symbol of two trees. We descend into mortality to partake of the fruit of the tree of knowledge. Cast out of God's immediate presence, we learn by our own experiences. It is through our agency and our choices that we partake of this fruit and thereby fall individually. This life is where the battle occurs. You are engaged in it every day. We can learn and understand things in our head, but it is quite another thing to learn through experience. For instance, we can read and learn about forgiveness, but we really come to understand it when someone injures us and we have to forgive them. It is the same with faith and many other principles that we can gain here while outside of God's presence. The key here is to not walk alone. We desperately need God's involvement and direction in our day-to-day lives in order to accomplish and learn everything we were sent here for.

Having fallen, our task now is to find our way back to the tree of life, or a return to God's presence. The fruit of this tree is "most desirable above all other fruits; yea, and it is the greatest of all the gifts of God" (1 Nephi 15:36). Down here in mortality, there are plenty of ways to get lost—but only one path back to the tree of life. It ran alongside the rod of iron in Lehi's dream. Nephi explained that the rod of iron was the word of God and that if we hold fast to it we will not perish (see 1 Nephi 15:24). He interpreted many of the other elements of his father's dream, but didn't explain the path until the very end of his writings. Then, he devoted two full chapters to it (see 2 Nephi 31 and 32). The path is the doctrine of

Christ. It leads to eternal life (see 2 Nephi 31:18). And as Nephi testified, *there is no other way* (see 2 Nephi 31:21).

The doctrine of Christ isn't just another Church program or part of the gospel. It is *the* path. There is no other way back to God. So this doctrine is critical to each of us! Christ's part is to save us through His Atonement. Our part is outlined in the doctrine of Christ, which contains the Father's saving instructions to us. We will discuss more of how this ties into and with the temple later, but the very best preparation you can make for the temple is to learn, follow, and live the doctrine of Christ in your life. The temple will then strengthen and help you further along in that path. But we will never outgrow the basic doctrine of Christ in this life.

HOMEWORK

1. Carefully study the doctrine of Christ as outlined in the Book of Mormon (2 Nephi 31 and 32; 3 Nephi 11 and 27). It summarizes our path back to Christ.
2. How fully have you implemented this doctrine in your life? What could you still work on?

Chapter 3
FAITH

The first principle of the gospel is faith. We often speak of faith, but what exactly is it? How do we get it, and how does it grow? Why is it so important? These questions are worth careful thought and consideration. We will briefly discuss them here, but you should spend some time on your own studying and pondering the topic of faith.

The scriptures have a great deal to say about faith. For example, we cannot please God unless we have faith (see Hebrews 11:6). Why is that? One reason may be that God can't bless us with all that He would like to unless we have faith. In fact, you cannot be saved unless and until you have sufficient faith (see Moroni 7:26, 38). Faith, therefore, is crucial. So how do you develop it?

Initially, faith comes from hearing the *word of God* (see Romans 10:17). This is the seed Alma talked about (see Alma 32). Once the seed is planted, the continuing word of God is required to nourish faith and help it grow. This is one reason it is so important to study and ponder the scriptures. Spend time with the word of God. Faith is part of the power that begins to flow into your life from a careful study of the Book of Mormon.[9]

However, the scriptures are not the only way that we receive the *word of God*. God's word also includes the answers we receive from Him in response to our personal prayers. On the path of discipleship, each of us can and should receive our own promises from Him. The temple is another place you will receive the word of God. In the temple ordinances, you receive wonderful promises from Him given directly to you.

As God's word is planted in our hearts and faith sprouts and begins to grow, we will see the results. These results may start very small, but they will grow in time as we continue nurturing our faith. Eventually, miracles come because of faith (see Ether 12:12–18). And faith is how we obtain every good thing (see Moroni 7:20–21). In fact, the Lord tells us that He does not work in our lives unless we have faith: "For behold, I am God; and I am a God of miracles; and I will show unto the world that I am the same yesterday, today, and forever; and *I work not among the children of men save it be according to their faith*" (2 Nephi 27:23; emphasis added). If you don't see God's hand in your life then it may mean you don't have faith. If that is the case, go obtain it.

So is faith just belief? Or is it something more? The Apostle James taught that the devils also believe and tremble (see James 2:19). Faith therefore must be more than just belief. The devils obviously don't have faith. They know God exists but they are still lacking something. James gives us a clue as to what is missing. He says that faith without works is dead (James 2:20). It isn't enough to just believe in God. We must trust Him and His word enough to act upon it. Put most simply, faith is our belief put into action.

FAITH IN JESUS CHRIST

Notice, however, that the first principle of the gospel is not just faith, but specifically faith in the Lord Jesus Christ. It is not faith in ourselves. We must learn to trust Him and to have faith in Him. This might seem easy until He requires something of us that we don't want to do or that is difficult. It is one thing to trust in God when we are filled with the Spirit at a fireside or a testimony meeting, and it can be quite another when we are contemplating interrupting our life plans to serve a mission or when things seem to be going wrong and we don't seem to be getting answers to our earnest prayers. In those times, faith can be hard. It is easy to let our doubts and fears take over.

Our trust and confidence in our Savior must not only include faith in His promises and commandments, but also faith in His timing and His willingness to help us. Sometimes He requires us to take a step or two into the dark. We don't always see the end from the beginning. The light may not reappear until we have shown our faith by taking those first faltering steps. Yet if we will plant the seed and allow it to grow, faith can develop from a small seed into a mighty tree. The temple's teachings and blessings are a great help in the process.

During the early years of the Church, Joseph Smith and Sidney Rigdon prepared a series of lessons on faith. These lessons were called the *Lectures on Faith* and were accepted by the Church as part of the Doctrine and Covenants in 1835.[10] These lectures were given to help prepare the members for their upcoming endowment in the Kirtland Temple. In one sense, we could say the lectures were the original temple preparation manual. These early members needed to further develop their faith in order to be endowed with power as the Lord had promised (see D&C 95:8). The endowment was not simply additional ordinances, but was to be a rich Pentecostal-type outpouring of the Spirit and spiritual manifestations. The Saints needed faith in order to receive it.

THREE PREREQUISITES

The *Lectures on Faith* have important things to teach us about the doctrine of faith and are well worth studying in their entirety. They are good preparation for your future temple endowment as well. Consequently, we are going to highlight just a few of their key teachings here. In order for us to have faith, the lectures declare that three things are necessary:

1. The idea that God exists
2. A correct idea of His character and attributes
3. Knowledge that our course in life is according to His will[11]

If our salvation depends upon having faith, then these three things are critical for us to clearly understand.

Faith has to be based on truth to be effective. We can believe all day long in something that isn't true, but our faith in it will not yield any fruit. This is one reason we need to relentlessly seek truth all our lives. Once we understand that God exists, it is then critical to have a correct idea of God's character and His attributes. We need a correct picture of Him in our minds. Is He a stern, vengeful, intergalactic ruler too busy to be bothered with the likes of us? Or is He more like Santa Claus, a grandfatherly type who waits to grant our every wish? As ridiculous as both of these characterizations are, sometimes we reflect them in our approach to prayer and our relationship with Him. If we set them aside, the question remains: what is He really like?

GOD'S CHARACTER AND ATTRIBUTES

The best initial source for knowledge about God is the scriptures written by prophets who have met Him and conversed with Him face-to-face, as did Joseph Smith. They recorded their encounters for our benefit, so that we could begin to exercise faith and come to know God ourselves. Eventually our personal experiences with God will reinforce these same truths and our faith and trust in Him can ultimately come from our own knowledge. But it does not start out that way. So, let's consider some of the things the scriptures and prophets teach about our Heavenly Father and our Savior. There are six characteristics of God summarized in the Lectures on Faith.

1. *God is endless and everlasting.* The first truth is that God was God before the world was created and that He is still the same God after it was created (see Lecture 3:13). Without this belief, we could not exercise our faith in Him. For if we did not

> Believe Him to be [the] God, that is, the Creator and upholder of all things, [we] could not center [our] faith in Him for life and salvation, for fear there should be a greater than He, who would thwart all His plans, and He, like the gods of the heathen, would be unable to fulfill His promises; but seeing He is God over all, from everlasting to everlasting, the Creator and upholder of all things, no such fear can exist in the minds of those who put their trust in Him, so that in this respect their faith can be without wavering. (Lecture 3:19)

God is the creator of all things—worlds without number (see Moses 1:33). He has all knowledge, all power, and fulfills all His words (see Moses 4:30). In other words, God isn't experimenting with us. He knows what He is doing and knows how to save us. We can put our complete trust in Him and in His plan. He has testified, "For behold, this is my work and my glory—to bring to pass the immortality and eternal life of man" (Moses 1:39). You are at the heart of God's work.

2. *God is no respecter of persons* (see Lecture 3:17). Think about what that really means. It is so very different from what we see all around us in the world. Most all of us tend to be a *respecter of persons*, meaning we esteem people differently. There are people we regard very highly and others that we think less of. God isn't that way. All are important to Him. The temple endowment reminds us of this fact as we sit side by side dressed alike in white. The Book of Mormon likewise testifies: "the one being is as precious

in his sight as the other" (Jacob 2:21). "He inviteth them all to come unto him and partake of his goodness; and he denieth none that come unto him, black and white, bond and free, male and female . . . and all are alike unto God" (2 Nephi 26:33).

Nor does your Church calling matter in approaching the Lord. He invites *you* to come unto Him, to receive any blessing that any prophet or any other person before you has ever received from the Lord. Your bishop or your stake president or even an Apostle doesn't have some inherent advantage. All are alike before the Lord. All must come unto Him on the same terms and conditions. All must develop faith. Everyone must abide by the same laws to receive the blessings (see D&C 130:20–21). And "in every nation he [or she] that fears God and works righteousness is accepted of Him" (Lecture 3:17).

What then, if anything, will limit us in knowing Him? Only our own effort or lack thereof. "The extent of [our] knowledge, respecting His character and glory, will depend upon [our] diligence and faithfulness in seeking after Him" (Lecture 2:55). To a great extent, our relationship with the Lord is largely up to us. He will draw near unto us as we draw near unto Him (see D&C 88:63).

3. *God is merciful.* Once we realize that all have an equal opportunity to come unto the Lord, we then need to understand that He is also "merciful and gracious, slow to anger, abundant in goodness, and that He was so from everlasting, and will be to everlasting" (Lecture 3:14). All of us are so weak and frail and imperfect, yet He still loves us. In fact, the closer we draw to the Lord, the more we sense our individual weakness. Even stalwart Nephi exclaimed, "O wretched man that I am! Yea, my heart sorroweth because of my flesh; my soul grieveth because of mine iniquities" (2 Nephi 4:17). This isn't some kind of false modesty on Nephi's part. He keenly sensed his own inadequacy, despite his great spiritual experiences. Contrast his feelings with those of Laman and Lemuel who argued (and probably felt this same way about themselves); "we know that the people who were in the land of Jerusalem were a righteous people; for they kept the statutes and judgments of the Lord, and all his commandments, according to the law of Moses; wherefore, we know that they are a righteous people; and our father hath judged them" (1 Nephi 17:22). Pride limits our relationship with God, while humility enables it.

It may be that as you clearly sense your own weakness and sin, it is because you are nearer to God than you realize. Take comfort in the fact that He doesn't want to remember our sins (see D&C 58:42). He wants to forgive us (see Isaiah 1:18), heal us (see 3 Nephi 9:13), and give us eternal life (see 3 Nephi 9:14). Truly, our Savior is merciful and gracious and slow to anger. Because of that, we can come unto Him regardless of the sins, struggles, or challenges that we may face. Those very things may be, in fact, a gift to help us truly come unto Him in a deeper and more personal way than we ever could without them (see Ether 12:27). Have faith and trust in His goodness and unwavering love for you. Bring your burdens to Him. Believe His promise: "Come now, and let us reason together, saith the Lord: though your sins be as scarlet, they shall be as white as snow; though they be red like crimson, they shall be as wool" (Isaiah 1:18).

4. *God cannot lie.* Equally important to developing our faith is knowing that God is "a God of truth and cannot lie" (Lecture 3:16). When the brother of Jared met with the Lord on mount Shelem, he saw the Lord's finger and then asked the Lord to reveal Himself. Before doing so, Christ asked him a question: "Believest thou the words which I shall speak?" The brother of Jared responded, "Yea, Lord, I know that thou . . . art a God of truth, and canst not lie" (Ether 3:10–12). Without that knowledge, the brother of Jared could not have received the blessings that followed. Why that was the case? Why did the brother of Jared need that knowledge before being redeemed? And how had he gained it? Was it simply book learning? Or had he learned that God could not lie because of his own personal experiences in seeing the Lord's word fulfilled in his life?

Likewise, when we receive a promise from the Lord, we can have complete faith in its fulfillment, even if sometimes the blessing is manifest differently than we expected. The Lord's promises will always be fully vindicated. At times it is difficult to trust in the Lord's timing, especially when He has us wait. Abraham and Sarah received the promise of Isaac, decades before he was born. Long after her potential childbearing years had passed, Abraham and Sarah continued to believe and have faith in the Lord's promise (see Romans 4:18–21). There was no rational reason to believe, other than that God had given His word. Sarah was barren and past menopause. Still they believed, and eventually the promised blessing came.

The idea that He is a God of truth and cannot lie is equally necessary for us. Without this, we could not have full, unreserved confidence in His word. But having the idea that He cannot lie enables the minds of men to exercise faith in Him (see Lecture 3:22).

5. *God doesn't change* (see Lecture 3:15). "For he is the same yesterday, today, and forever; and the way is prepared for all men from the foundation of the world, if it so be that they repent and come unto him. For he that diligently seeketh shall find; and the mysteries of God shall be unfolded unto them, by the power of the Holy Ghost, as well in these times as in times of old, and as well in times of old as in times to come; wherefore, the course of the Lord is one eternal round" (1 Nephi 10:18–19). What God was yesterday, He still is today, and will still be tomorrow (see Lecture 3:21). The things He required of His Saints in the past will be the same that He requires of us today. The same blessings are available upon the same conditions. The gospel doesn't change.

6. *God is love* (see Lecture 3:18). Finally, and perhaps most important, you need to really know that God loves you. He loves you so much in fact that the scriptures can say "God is love" (1 John 4:8). Our Father showed the depth of that love by sending His Son to be our Savior. And Christ showed how much He loves you and how much you mean to Him by the things He suffered for you (see D&C 18:10). God's love is both universal and very personal. He loves everyone, but I also believe He loves us as completely and uniquely as though we were His only child. His love never ceases, falters, or fades. It is eternal. A parent's love may be the closest thing we experience in this life. In particular, a mother's love is great because of her suffering and her sacrifice for her children.

We see an example of this kind of love in the true-life story of Stacie Crimm. In March of 2011, Stacie had laughed and cried from joy upon learning that she was finally pregnant at the age of forty-one. It was a happy, miraculous moment, as doctors had previously told her that she would never be able to have a child. A few months later, however, she began experiencing severe headaches and double vision. A medical scan revealed that Stacie had an aggressive cancer spreading through her head and neck. Without treatment it would be terminal. Doctors informed her that the cancer could be treated with chemotherapy, but that would likely prove fatal for her baby. Stacie faced an excruciating choice: her life or her baby's.

She chose life for her baby, fully knowing that it would cost her her own. She declined the chemotherapy. Her one wish was that she would be able to live long enough to hold her newborn daughter.

One afternoon in mid-August, Stacie collapsed in her home and was rushed to the hospital. Another scan showed that the invasive tumor had spread and begun wrapping around her brain stem, slowly killing her. After two days in the hospital, Stacie's heart stopped. While medics rushed to resuscitate her, doctors decided it was best to deliver the premature baby, by C-section, even though it was weeks before the due date.

The delivery was successful—a two-pound, one-ounce girl named Dottie Mae, was rushed off to intensive care. Stacie was revived, but her health continued to deteriorate in the weeks following the birth. Both mother and daughter required constant medical attention and were kept apart. By this point, the cancer had paralyzed Stacie's throat making it hard for her to speak or to be understood. She often fell unconscious. In September, her heart stopped once again. She quit breathing and lay dying, but again the doctors were able to revive her.

Everyone knew that Stacie's remaining time was very short. They also knew of her wish. She had still not been able to hold her newborn daughter or count her tiny, perfect fingers or look into her blue eyes. A few days later, Stacie regained consciousness briefly. Nurses wheeled baby Dottie out of intensive care, down the hallway, and placed the tiny infant on her mother's chest. For several minutes, mother and daughter gazed into one another's eyes, while the nurses watched and wept. It was a sacred moment. No one said a word. Three days later, Stacie passed away.[12]

The love Stacie had for her baby is a type (or a reflection) of the love that Christ has for you. You can have complete faith and trust in Him because of His infinite love. I hope and pray that you have felt it from time to time in your life.

OUR COURSE IN LIFE

Returning to our discussion on faith, the six attributes we've reviewed are found over and over in the scriptures. We must understand them in order to begin to come unto God and exercise faith in Him. Our trust and confidence needs to be based on an understanding of these attributes. Otherwise our faith will be weak and imperfect.[13]

Once we begin to understand God's character, the third thing we need in order to truly exercise faith in Him is the knowledge that our course in life is according to His will. At a minimum, this means that we are trying to keep the commandments and to live the gospel. But it may also mean something more. The decisions that you face in your life and the paths that you choose need to be led by the Lord. We need to trust in Him and lean not unto our own understanding—enabling Him to direct our lives (see Proverbs 3:5–6).

The opportunities and challenges each of us face are unique. The things the Lord would like you to do and the people you can bless are also uniquely yours. You need the guidance of His Spirit to be able to do His will in your life. Even if that requires you to sometimes be led, like Nephi, not knowing everything beforehand (see 1 Nephi 4:6). When we know we are living right and we are on the Lord's errand, we can have faith and confidence in Him and His willingness to help us. Then we can join Paul in declaring, "I can do all things through Christ which strengtheneth me" (Philippians 4:13).

If there are things amiss in your life, take care of them. If you aren't certain that your path in life is what God would want or are unsure of your standing before Him, then make that a matter of prayer until you receive answers and direction. Get things right so that you can begin to completely exercise your faith and confidence in Him. Faith is power that causes us to act. Our direction needs to be set by the Lord. Like the oil for the virgin's lamps, faith is not something that someone else can give you (see Matthew 25:9). You must pay the required price to develop and obtain your own faith. Faith then becomes a power through which the Lord can work miracles in your life (see Jacob 4:7; Ether 12).

Recognize up front that as you begin to walk by faith, you will also encounter opposition and your faith will be tried. This should not come as a surprise. The scriptures testify that we receive no witness until after the trial of our faith (see Ether 12:6). Or another way to phrase it is that we never have a perfect knowledge at first. Faith requires us to act even when we aren't totally certain. It is only by taking these steps of faith into the dark that we eventually learn why they were required. By divine design, we obtain knowledge only after first exercising faith. Our faith can only grow as it is stretched and tried and proven. In fact, Peter testified that the trial of our faith is more precious to us than gold, because the end result of our faith will be the salvation of our souls (see 1 Peter 1:7, 9).

Nephi's life is a great example of how to develop faith. His record begins when his father came home and told the family to pack their bags. I can imagine how most teenage boys would have reacted to that kind of news. In all fairness, Nephi, too, had some doubts at first. But, unlike his brothers, Nephi took his questions to the Lord (see 1 Nephi 2:16). He recorded that the Lord softened his heart so that he believed the words of his father. The Lord would not have needed to send the Spirit to soften Nephi's heart if he hadn't had doubts and concerns about what was happening. Nephi returned from his initial experience with the spiritual reassurance that they were indeed on the Lord's errand. He gained the third element needed for faith. He knew their path was in harmony with the Lord's will.

Because of the Lord's assurance, when Lehi received instructions to return to Jerusalem for the plates, Nephi responded immediately, "I will go and do" (1 Nephi 3:7). He immediately accepted that the commandment was from the Lord and expressed his faith that the Lord would help them. He acted in faith based upon his earlier assurance from the Lord that they truly were on His errand.

Now, we all know the rest of the story. The point is this: Nephi and his brothers failed twice in their attempts to obtain the plates. In all of that time, there was no further evidence that the Lord was with them. Nephi's faith was being tried. In fact, the Lord didn't intervene until they had given up all their wealth and it was apparent that the entire mission was doomed to failure. Nephi's brothers were so angry at everything that they were beating him with a stick. At that point, the angel of the Lord stepped in with help and the miracle occurred as a result of Nephi's faith. This entire experience reinforced and increased Nephi's faith.

If you step back and look at the entire incident, you find a pattern emerges, demonstrating the process by which faith grows. The cycle often begins with a question, confusion, or doubt. When this is taken to God, a spiritual witness or answer is received. Later the opposition shows up in full force. For a time, failure may appear imminent. At that point, there is always a temptation to question or doubt the earlier answer or revelation. This is a trial of faith. If you hold true to the earlier answer and press forward, the Lord eventually intervenes, miracles occur, and faith increases. You can then walk forward with increased faith. You can also expect the pattern to repeat.

We get a glimpse into how Nephi persevered through the opposition once the angel departed. Immediately, Laman and Lemuel began to complain once again. They feared and doubted, yet Nephi reminded them of the experience of Moses and the Israelites when they left Egypt (see 1 Nephi 4:2–3). He likened the scriptures from the past to their present situation. He knew he was on the Lord's errand and fully expected the Lord to deliver him, just as the Lord had blessed Moses and the ancient Israelites. We should do the same. The story of obtaining the brass plates isn't included in the Book of Mormon for the purpose of knowing the

Nephites had the scriptures with them and how they obtained them. Rather, it helps us recognize this same pattern in our own life experiences. As we seek to do the Lord's will, we can expect the same response when we exercise the same faith. This is how faith grows and develops.

Nephi's experience of deliverance is another witness added to that of the ancient Israelites of the Lord's power to deliver us, even when death or failure appear to be the only future ahead of us. Laman and Lemuel, like the ancient Israelites fleeing the Egyptians, forgot all of the prior miracles the Lord had performed for them and could only see the immediate threat of Laban looming in front of them.

Even after the angel reaffirms that the Lord is indeed with them and promises them deliverance, Nephi still wasn't given all of the answers. He was again required to take a few steps of faith into the dark before the path became apparent. He records simply, "I was led by the Spirit, not knowing beforehand the things which I should do" (1 Nephi 4:6).

Nephi walked by faith. You will also be required to walk by faith at many points in your own life. Without faith, you cannot be endowed with power from on high. Without faith, you cannot receive the blessings the Lord wants to give you. And, unless you acquire faith, you cannot follow the path outlined in the temple endowment.

HOMEWORK

1. Obtain a copy of and study the *Lectures on Faith*. Faith is a critical part of your preparation for receiving and then living your endowment. These lectures were prepared by Joseph Smith to help us understand and gain the faith necessary to lay hold upon eternal life.

2. Read the talk "'Cast Not Away Therefore Your Confidence,'" by Elder Jeffrey R. Holland (see *Ensign*, March 2000; available online). This talk masterfully illustrates the process of pushing through our doubts and the trials of our faith to obtain God's blessings.

Chapter 4
REPENTANCE

*R*epentance is a word that may be very misunderstood, but it is a crucial topic for each of us to understand. Searching for the word *repent* in the scriptures reveals something very interesting. The word *repent* occurs:

39 times in the Old Testament,
36 times in the New Testament,
82 times in the Doctrine and Covenants, and
220 times in the Book of Mormon.

Clearly one of the central themes of the Book of Mormon is repentance. If you accept Joseph Smith's testimony that we will get nearer to God by abiding by the precepts of the Book of Mormon than by those of any other book, then the message of the Book of Mormon is critical for us.[14] Repentance is a key part of that message.

The Heart of Repentance

Repentance begins with getting our heart right before God. It is turning to face Him and putting Him first in our lives. Each of us can begin to do that regardless of the sins or weaknesses we struggle with. In fact, a big part of repentance is really filling our life with God and seeking to do His will. The very process of doing that will begin to crowd out and eliminate many of the bad things we sometimes struggle with. The Book of Mormon plainly testifies that only the meek and lowly in heart are acceptable to

God (see Moroni 7:44). This truth is at the core of repentance. To further illustrate this point, please permit me to recast one of the Savior's parables in a more modern setting.

This is a story about two Laurels, Brooke and Rachel, living in the same ward. Brooke seemed to have everything going for her. She was beautiful, had a fun personality, and was usually happy. Brooke served as the Laurel class president, and most of the girls really liked her. Brooke was also popular at school. She enjoyed coming to church and visiting with her friends. Brooke tried very hard to live all of the guidelines in the *For the Strength of Youth* pamphlet and to keep the standards of the Church. She was glad she didn't have any major sins in her life like so many other kids in her school.

Rachel, on the other hand, struggled with her self-esteem. She wasn't very popular but had a few close friends. She often wished she were more confident, more like Brooke. Rachel also tried very hard to live the Church standards but often made mistakes. She struggled with some sins in her life. At times she really got down on herself, especially when she messed up and fell into old bad habits. Life was a battle for her. Rachel often felt socially awkward and didn't always fit in. Though she was pretty, Rachel had never felt really beautiful. It was easy for the other kids to overlook her.

One day, their Laurel class scheduled a visit to the temple to do baptisms for the dead. Everyone was excited to go and participate. It required several hours of travel to reach the nearest temple, so the class planned an all-day excursion. As the day drew near, Rachel met with her bishop to get a recommend. She had made good progress in her life, and her bishop felt she was ready to go to the temple again. She was excited about her new recommend and looked forward to the trip. It had been a long time since she had been to the temple. Unfortunately, Satan and his minions were also aware of Rachel's progress. As the temple day approached, they worked overtime on her. The night before the trip they succeeded in tempting her to relapse into an old habit. Rachel felt terrible and discouraged. She had worked so hard and now it felt like she was back to square one.

During the long drive, Brooke chatted happily with the other girls. The trip passed quickly for them. Rachel, however, sat mostly quiet. No one paid her much attention or noticed the quiet turmoil inside. She wrestled with what to do. No one knew of her relapse. She carried her new recommend in her purse. It would be so easy to slip inside the temple with all of the other girls. But in her heart, Rachel knew she couldn't do it. By the time the group arrived, she knew what to do. She briefly explained that she didn't feel worthy to go inside and would wait for the others outside on the temple grounds.

Brooke and the others eagerly entered the temple. Brooke secretly wondered what Rachel had done. She and some of the other girls whispered about it as they went inside. Why was Rachel not worthy to enter the temple? Maybe it was a good thing that they didn't always include Rachel. After all, they wouldn't want any of her bad habits rubbing off on them, even if they weren't sure exactly what those habits were. Brooke speculated as to the answer. She felt proud that she was worthy of a temple recommend and that she didn't have any big sins in her life. She was keeping the commandments. She was a wonderful, living example of the *For the Strength of Youth* standards. She was so glad that she wasn't like Rachel.

Rachel waited outside on the temple grounds. She wasn't sure that she was even worthy to be there, but she desperately felt her need for her Savior. She wanted to feel close to Him again. As she waited on the beautiful temple grounds, she pled with the Lord for forgiveness and for mercy for her own sins. She asked for strength to overcome her weakness and to be able to follow her Savior's will. Finally, she prayed for Brooke and for the other girls in her class. Maybe they didn't mean to exclude her or leave her out. They probably didn't notice how they ignored her, but Rachel asked the Lord to forgive them and to have mercy on them as well. They needed Him just as much as she did. And being aware of her own burden and mistakes, she could more easily overlook theirs.

On the drive home that day, Rachel again sat quietly. This time, however, her soul was filled with peace. Brooke and the other girls again chatted amiably. But inside, Brooke still wondered what Rachel had done. *Best to keep some distance*, she thought and turned back to her friends. One of the other Laurels thought, *Maybe someone should have waited outside with Rachel. But then again, it really is Rachel's own fault. She deserved what she got for not living the standards.*

At the same time, the angels in heaven noted that Rachel had been forgiven for her mistakes. They wondered why Brooke hadn't noticed how absent the Spirit was in her life. Would she ever become aware of her own pride, gossiping, faultfinding, and lack of love and compassion for others? In so many ways, her life was good. But her heart was far from her Lord, and she was very blind to it. She was failing to truly love others and minister to them. The angels prayed that she would eventually come to see that her own need for her Savior was every bit as great as Rachel's need. And that eventually, Brooke might receive the same forgiveness and the same peace and love in her own life.

Now, I have taken some liberty in recasting this parable in a more modern setting, but hopefully to illustrate an important point: no matter how *righteous* or how *hopeless* we may feel, we are all in desperate need of our Savior. We are never going to overcome the natural man or transcend this telestial sphere without His help and grace. Or, as Aaron testified to the Lamanite king, "since man had fallen he could not merit anything of himself" (Alma 22:14). In other words, we are never going to be good enough on our own. Never. Ever. The first step of repentance is to awaken to our own worthless and fallen state and our need for Christ (see Mosiah 4:2).

King Benjamin's people were living basically good lives and had gathered at the temple. But after hearing the words of the angel delivered by King Benjamin, they "viewed themselves in their own carnal state, even less than the dust of the earth" (Mosiah 4:2). They saw the truth and cried for mercy from their Savior. The scriptures record the result: "The Spirit of the Lord came upon them, and they were filled with joy, having received a remission of their sins, and having peace of conscience because of the exceeding faith which they had in Jesus Christ" (Mosiah 4:3). It was because of their faith. If you don't have these same blessings in your life it may be because you haven't yet understood the truth about yourself and God.

Brooke hadn't reached a point in her life where she could see and understand this truth. She trusted in her own "righteousness" and failed to see her equally great need for her Savior. He would wait patiently until she did. Because of her circumstances and struggles, Rachel was beginning to see her dependence upon Christ, and, as a result, her relationship with Him was growing. In His eyes, she was further along in her journey. Rachel was gaining a broken heart and contrite spirit.

This point is important enough that we should also consider the Savior's original parable:

> Two men went up into the temple to pray; the one a Pharisee [Pharisees were well respected and looked up to as religious leaders. This is Brooke in our modern version.], and the other a publican. [Publicans were tax collectors. They were often despised and looked down upon by others—in other words, our Rachel.] The Pharisee stood and prayed thus with himself, [notice that he is praying with "himself." God doesn't even acknowledge his prayer.] God, I thank thee, that I am not as other

men are, extortioners, unjust, adulterers, or even as this publican. I fast twice in the week, I give tithes of all that I possess. [Christ doesn't deny that the Pharisee is actually doing these good things, but he is still missing the core of the gospel.]

And the publican, standing afar off, would not lift up so much as his eyes unto heaven, but smote upon his breast, saying, God be merciful to me a sinner. I tell you, this man went down to his house justified rather than the other: for every one that exalteth himself shall be abased; and he that humbleth himself shall be exalted. (Luke 18:10–14)

Regardless of where we are at in our own individual journey, we all desperately need our Savior. We are never going to *save* ourselves. Repentance is not so much about where we are at in this moment as which direction we are facing. Turn and face Christ.

Once we have gained a broken heart and a contrite spirit, we must strive to keep our hearts soft and open and not harden them again. King Benjamin testified that in order to be filled with the love of God and to retain a remission of our sins, we need to "always retain in remembrance, the greatness of God, and your own nothingness, and his goodness and long-suffering towards you, unworthy creatures, and humble yourselves even in the depths of humility, calling on the name of the Lord daily, and standing steadfastly in the faith" (Mosiah 4:11; see also verse 12). This is the heart of true repentance.

Viewing ourselves as God's chosen people or as a *royal generation* can interfere with seeing our true condition and absolute need for God. No matter how *righteous* we are, everyone falls short. Or as Lehi put it, "by the law [we] are cut off" (see 2 Nephi 2:5). We will never save ourselves solely through our obedience. Obedience is important and does serve a couple of vital purposes, one of which is to keep us spiritually safe and avoid the awful consequences of sin. So just to be clear, I am not saying that the standards and commandments are not important. They provide important spiritual safeguards and guides that can help us avoid painful and awful consequences from sin. But if our observance of those standards makes us proud or judgmental of others or blind to our own need for Christ, then our very obedience can become a stumbling block. Consider the following experience from our Savior's life:

One of the Pharisees desired him that he would eat with him. And he went into the Pharisee's house, and sat down to meat.

And, behold, a woman in the city, which was a sinner, when she knew that Jesus sat at meat in the Pharisee's house, brought an alabaster box of ointment,

And stood at his feet behind him weeping, and began to wash his feet with tears, and did wipe them with the hairs of her head, and kissed his feet, and anointed them with the ointment.

Now when the Pharisee which had bidden him saw it, he spake within himself, saying, This man, if he were a prophet, would have known who and what manner of woman this is that toucheth him: for she is a sinner.

And Jesus answering said unto him, Simon, I have somewhat to say unto thee. And he saith, Master, say on.

There was a certain creditor which had two debtors: the one owed five hundred pence, and the other fifty.

And when they had nothing to pay, he frankly forgave them both. Tell me therefore, which of them will love him most?

Simon answered and said, I suppose that he, to whom he forgave most. And he said unto him, Thou hast rightly judged.

And he turned to the woman, and he said unto Simon, Seest thou this woman? I entered into thine house, thou gavest me no water for my feet: but she hath washed my feet with tears, and wiped them with the hairs of her head.

Thou gavest me no kiss: but this woman since the time I came in hath not ceased to kiss my feet.

My head with oil thou didst not anoint: but this woman hath anointed my feet with ointment.

Wherefore I say unto thee, Her sins, which are many, are forgiven; for she loved much: but to whom little is forgiven, the same loveth little.

And he said unto her, Thy sins are forgiven. (Luke 7:36–48)

Simon saw himself as more *righteous* and better than the woman. She was unworthy. He despised her and couldn't believe that the Savior would allow her to touch Him or that He would associate with her. And so Jesus patiently explained how He viewed the situation. We can't always accurately judge. Sometimes those who have sinned, struggled, and repented, emerge from their pain with a genuine compassion and greater love for others. This woman, a known sinner, was forgiven and cleansed. Simon was not. The irony is that by our standards, Simon probably had in fact lived a "better" life, but his heart hadn't yet been softened and changed by God's love. Hopefully, he repented.

We usually don't see what lies in another person's heart. We may not be fully aware of their circumstances or the burdens they carry. The beautiful thing about becoming one of Christ's disciples is that He does not ask us to judge but rather to bear one another's burdens. Life isn't some great competition with only a few spots at the top. We are here to help and serve each other in our journey, not to be better than others. We should keep our focus on the two great commandments: to love God and to love our neighbor as ourselves. In that one sentence is a truth so profound that we can spend the remainder of our lives trying to learn and live it better. Others should be able to recognize us as one of His disciples by the love we demonstrate to others (see John 13:35). Stop and think about your life for a minute. How could you better love God and His children? In fact, I believe this love is at the very heart of one of the covenants we make in the temple. (For more on this, see chapter 9.)

RECEIVING FORGIVENESS AND FORGIVING OTHERS

One starting point to showing more love is forgiving others. Once forgiven, we in turn must forgive. Christ taught this principle in a parable. A king had a servant who owed him ten thousand talents. When the servant could not pay, the king forgave the debt. Later, the same servant went out and found another servant who owed him a hundred pence and would not forgive him in like manner but rather cast him into prison. When the king learned of this he was angry with the first servant and delivered him up until he should likewise pay his much greater debt (see Matthew 18:23–34). Christ concluded, "so likewise shall my heavenly Father do also unto you, if ye from your hearts forgive not every one his brother their trespasses" (Matthew 18:35).

This can sometimes be difficult, especially when we have suffered real pain or loss by another's actions. But in forgiving and praying for others, even our enemies, we begin to act in the role of intercessor for them. We come to understand our Lord, because we are emulating His behavior.

Our Master taught by word and example:

> And as ye would that men should do to you, do ye also to them likewise.
>
> For if ye love them which love you, what thank have ye? for sinners also love those that love them.

And if ye do good to them which do good to you, what thank have ye? for sinners also do even the same. . . .

But love ye your enemies, and do good, and lend, hoping for nothing again; and your reward shall be great, and ye shall be the children of the Highest: for he is kind unto the unthankful and to the evil.

Be ye therefore merciful, as your Father also is merciful.

Judge not, and ye shall not be judged: condemn not, and ye shall not be condemned: forgive, and ye shall be forgiven:

Give, and it shall be given unto you; good measure, pressed down, and shaken together, and running over, shall men give into your bosom. For with the same measure that ye mete withal it shall be measured to you again. (Luke 6:31–38)

Joseph Smith echoed these teachings of our Savior, "If you will not accuse me, I will not accuse you. If you will throw a cloak of charity over my sins, I will over yours—for charity covereth a multitude of sins."[15] We must forgive others' wrongs against us in order for God to forgive us in return. "Wherefore, I say unto you, that ye ought to forgive one another; for he that forgiveth not his brother [or sister] his trespasses standeth condemned before the Lord; for there remaineth in him the greater sin" (D&C 64:9). Of course, forgiveness doesn't mean that you must allow someone to continue to harm you. There may be people in our lives that aren't a good influence on us or who drag us down or are harmful. In such cases we may need to discontinue or limit our association with them. The Savior also taught that we should cast such things away from us (see Matthew 5:30).

OBEDIENCE

Obedience to the commandments is also important. Sometimes people feel the commandments are restrictive. In reality, the commandments don't hold us back; rather, it is our sins that limit us. Years ago I served as a teachers quorum adviser. One of our young men loved sports, especially soccer. He played competitively and worked very hard at becoming a good soccer player. He practiced regularly, exercised daily, and watched his diet carefully. He also lived the Word of Wisdom. Sometimes he felt a little discouraged that despite all of these things, other young men seemed to do better in the sport. Some of his teammates broke the Word of Wisdom and other commandments but still outperformed him on the soccer field. In his mind, this seemed unfair and wrong.

CHAPTER 4

We don't always receive an immediate blessing for obedience or an immediate consequence for disobedience to God's laws. But the natural consequences eventually follow. I explained to this young man that in some ways our lives are like a farm gate or a door. There isn't much movement or much difference near the hinge (maybe a few inches), but as you move out away from the hinge toward the end of the door, there is huge movement (many feet). Life is similar. When we are young there may not seem to be much difference between a teenage girl who is living the commandments and one who is not. Life is still near the hinges. But with our course left unchecked, as we move out a few years or decades into life, we find these things make a great difference in our lives. The commandments are given to bless and protect us.

As we strive to be obedient, sometimes it is easy to get down on ourselves when we sin or make mistakes. We need to learn from these experiences, and recognize that the Lord knows we are going to make mistakes. Still it can be genuinely discouraging to discover that we aren't as strong as we believed or that a sin we thought we had overcome has popped up once again. If you ever feel that way, I hope you will think about and remember a little analogy. Imagine holding two coins in your hand: one is bright, shiny, and new; the other is tarnished, dull, and covered with dirt to the point that it is almost hard to recognize it. But if I take them down to the store, they both have exactly the same value! Even if we fall flat on our face, the Lord doesn't abandon us or discard us. We still have the same value to Him. Because of His love, He wants to clean us up. If we repent, He won't leave us until we are shiny and new. Remember He testified that even if our sins are as scarlet, they can become as white as snow (see Isaiah 1:18).

So, if repentance is the good news, why does it sometimes carry a negative connotation? And if the Lord has totally compensated for our sins and is quick and willing to forgive, then why is repentance so hard at times? In part, it is because real change can be difficult. Sin is addictive and habit-forming. Habits gained over a lifetime can become chains that bind. It requires faith to repent. In this way the two principles are linked. As we exercise faith in Christ, we gain the power to repent (see Moroni 7:33–34).

We all struggle with bad habits. Some of us don't control our tempers or our tongues. Others of us wrestle with bodily appetites or other weaknesses. We mess up then swear to never do it again only to find ourselves repeating the same behavior later. At times it may be tempting to just give up and conclude, "I'll never change." Whether through our own sins or through situations in life, we eventually find ourselves in circumstances that are beyond our own ability to control. We find ourselves in some form of bondage. The Atonement is our only way out.

JUSTIFICATION AND SANCTIFICATION

It is through the Atonement that we receive forgiveness for our sins. But it is also through the Atonement that we receive the strength to forsake and overcome them. Our willpower alone is not enough. We will never be enough on our own! It does require all of our faith and all of our best efforts, but in the end it also requires Christ reaching down to us in grace to deliver us (see Mosiah 7:33). This will never happen, however, until we really, truly want the sin out of our life, even more than we want it in our life. And we are willing to pay any price ourselves to be rid of it. Those who understand this best are perhaps those who are recovering addicts (from drugs, alcohol, porn, and so on). But the principle applies to all of us.[16]

The scriptures refer to these two different functions of the Atonement as justification and sanctification. We are justified when we are forgiven and justice is satisfied. Sanctification, however, is something more. It goes beyond justification and involves forsaking the sin and becoming holy. It is the process of putting off the natural man and becoming a saint. The Atonement is at the heart of both processes. To illustrate the difference, we might think of a criminal who "pays his debt" to society by suffering in prison. He leaves prison justified. Justice can be satisfied by his prison sentence, but his behavior isn't necessarily reformed. Prison hasn't automatically made him a better person. He may return to the same behavior and poor choices. Sanctification is more than just receiving forgiveness—it is the process of becoming holy and covered by Christ's grace.

Why then can repentance and overcoming a bad habit be so difficult at times? I believe it is for a couple of reasons. One is so that we truly learn humility and to rely upon our Savior (see Ether 12:27), rather than relying upon our own strength. How often do we as Church members try to "save" ourselves? Another reason that we sometimes struggle so much before being freed from a sin is perhaps so we value the gift that is given us and don't revert back. We read of many whose repentance was so thorough, so complete (and probably so costly and difficult) that they were sanctified and could only look upon sin with abhorrence (see Alma 13:11–12).

Elder Bruce C. Hafen in his book, *The Broken Heart*, observes two common problems among the youth in the Church. On the one hand, some youth feel that they are *entitled* to a few "freebies" and then they will hurry up and repent before going on a mission or going to the temple or some other event that requires them to clean up their act. On the other hand, some are striving valiantly and are so hard on themselves for every mistake that they honestly feel they will never be good enough and will never make it back.[17]

On the surface these two groups seem to be polar opposites. However, on closer examination, they are actually two different sides to the same coin. Both groups suffer from a fundamental misunderstanding of and lack of appreciation for the Atonement. The first "no big deal" group severely underestimates the serious nature of their sins and has no appreciation for the price the Savior has paid for them. The second group also completely misses the Atonement by trying to save themselves or by believing that they have to be *worthy* or that they have to do enough good deeds before the Savior can step in to save them.

The truth is that only the meek and lowly in heart are acceptable to God (see Moroni 7:44). Real repentance begins there. Acquire a meek and lowly heart. Set aside your pride, and reach out to your Savior. It is only by His Atonement that we are saved (see Mosiah 4:7–8). And that is equally true of the *best* and of the *worst* among us.

REPENTANCE IS A LIFELONG PROCESS

As you begin the process of eliminating the bad from your life and gaining the good, you soon realize that repentance is a lifelong process. It is not just for *sinners*, but for *saints* as well. As we become more obedient, we gain further light and knowledge. Our understanding increases. The scriptures testify, "he that keepeth his commandments receiveth truth and light, until he is glorified in truth and knoweth all things" (D&C 93:28). The opposite is also true, "that wicked one cometh and taketh away light and truth, through disobedience, from the children of men, and because of the tradition of their fathers" (D&C 93:39). We gain light through obedience and lose it through disobedience and false traditions.

As our light increases, we must then change to reflect the further light and knowledge we have gained. To repent is to draw closer to God and eliminate those things that keep us from Him. It is a lifelong process of becoming more and more and more like our Savior—of doing as He would have us do, saying what He would have us say, and thinking as He would have us think. "That which is of God is light; and he that receiveth light, and continueth in God, receiveth more light; and that light groweth brighter and brighter until the perfect day" (D&C 50:24). In this world, things don't simply stay static. We are either moving forward or backward, gaining or losing light.

Repentance requires action. We can study the first principles and ordinances of the gospel—faith, repentance, baptism, and so on—and we can understand them intellectually, or in theory, but we don't truly understand them until we live them. Christ taught if we will *do* His will, then we shall *know* of the doctrine (see John 7:17). Obediently doing precedes fully understanding. It is in the actual living of gospel principles that we finally learn them. It is one thing to read about the second great commandment to love our neighbors, and a completely greater thing to actually learn to love them. We learn by first studying and then doing. It takes both. This shouldn't surprise us because it is the same process with any endeavor in life. We can study how to play the guitar, but we actually learn how by practicing, making mistakes, and starting over until we finally get it.

Lehi taught that we are all given sufficient light to know good from evil. We all have some portion of God's law. But because we all make mistakes constantly, we are condemned by the law, not justified by it (see 2 Nephi 2:5). That includes everyone except little children and those who are not accountable. None of us can ever hope to be good enough or to do enough to earn our way back on our own merits (see Alma 22:14). There is only one way out of our dilemma: the Holy Messiah who "offereth himself a sacrifice for sin, to answer the ends of the law, unto *all* those *who have a broken heart and a contrite spirit*; and unto *none else* can the ends of the law be answered" (2 Nephi 2:7; emphasis added). Only Christ can save you. However, you must have a broken heart and a contrite spirit in order for Him to do so.

The Lord taught Alma, "Marvel not that all mankind, yea, men and women, all nations, kindreds, tongues and people, must be born again; yea, *born of God*, changed from their carnal and fallen state, to a state of righteousness, being *redeemed of God, becoming his sons and daughters*. And thus they become new creatures; and unless they do this, they can in nowise inherit the kingdom of God" (Mosiah 27:25–26; emphasis added). Alma further testified that unless we are born again we must be cast off (see Mosiah 27:27). Alma's rebirth required him to repent "nigh unto death" and then came about only because of the Lord's mercy (Mosiah 27:28).

Repentance is the good news of the gospel. Our weakness is a gift from God (see Ether 12:27). Whether that gift proves to be a blessing or a curse is largely up to us. If we allow our weakness to fully bring us unto Christ in the depths of humility, then it will prove to be a great blessing, and Christ will heal us. On the other hand, our weakness can carry us far from Christ and His gospel. The choice is ours. We can stubbornly insist on relying upon our own efforts; harden our hearts and refuse the blessings offered us; or turn to Christ for mercy, healing, and relief. He pleads with us to come unto Him and warns: "For behold, I God, have suffered these things for all, that they might not suffer if they would repent; But if they would not repent they must suffer even as I" (D&C 19:16–17).

Each one of us faces some kind of battle. No one is exempt. You're not alone in your individual struggle. Choose to bring your burden to the Lord. Let Him cover you with His Atonement.

HOMEWORK

1. How is the condition of your heart? Do you have a broken heart and contrite spirit? Are you more like Brooke or Rachel? What could you change in your life to grow closer to Christ?
2. What do you need to repent of in your life?

Chapter 5
GOSPEL ORDINANCES

*O*rdinances provide access to the Atonement. The third article of faith states, "We believe that through the Atonement of Christ, all mankind may be saved, by obedience to the laws and ordinances of the Gospel" (Articles of Faith 1:3). From this we learn that three things are necessary for our salvation: the Atonement, the laws, and the ordinances. Obedience to gospel laws is essential, but the scriptures also testify that we are cut off by the law and not saved by it (see 2 Nephi 2:5). Our obedience is imperfect and falls short. We all need access to the Atonement. Ordinances help bridge this gap. They are the means the Lord has established for many of the blessings of the Atonement to flow into our lives. They are crucial. We cannot be saved without them (see, for example, John 3:5, Mark 16:16, 1 Peter 3:21, 3 Nephi 11:33, D&C 84:74). Through ordinances and the associated covenants, the power of the Atonement is activated in our lives.

BAPTISM

Baptism is the first saving ordinance of the gospel and is the next part of the doctrine of Christ. Our resurrected Lord testified repeatedly to the Nephites of the absolute necessity of baptism for salvation (see 3 Nephi 11:33–34, 37–38; 27:16, 20). We prepare for this ordinance through sincere, heartfelt repentance.

However, if you had never seen a baptism before, it might seem a little strange without some explanation or understanding of what it meant. Why is that person being dunked under water? It is the same with the sacrament. A person attending our Sunday worship services for the first time might wonder, why are all these people eating little pieces of bread in the middle of this meeting? And you may feel similarly with the ordinances of the temple. The temple ordinances themselves are simple but might seem a little odd until you have become familiar with them.

With any of the ordinances, the greater our understanding, the more our appreciation for them can grow. Over time they can become very beautiful and meaningful in our lives. So it is important to come to understand the temple ordinances on a deeper level.

THREE PARTS OF ORDINANCES

Most gospel ordinances have three components: 1) a covenant with associated blessings; 2) an external physical action; and 3) symbolic teachings. With baptism, the covenant we make is to take upon us the Lord's name and to follow Him. It is to keep His commandments, to love one another, and to bear one another's burdens (see Mosiah 18:8). We agree to live the gospel. The initial blessing of baptism is that of having our sins remitted (see Mark 1:4). Other future blessings are also promised. Baptism is the gate leading to eternal life (see 2 Nephi 31:8–9). Receiving this future blessing depends upon our faithfulness to the covenant made in the ordinance.

Covenants are much more than two-way promises; they have the potential to create sacred, binding relationships (see Mosiah 5:6–7). It is by making and keeping covenants that we become sons and daughters of Christ. (For a more in-depth discussion of covenants, please see chapter 1 of *Understanding Your Endowment*. Because the topic is covered thoroughly there, we won't spend time on it here.)

Ordinances also involve some physical action on our part. Ordinances are designed by and offered from God. We accept them by participating through the physical action (for example, eating the bread, going under the water, and so on). These physical actions are important—they witness to God and to others our personal acceptance of His covenant and are an outward expression of an inward commitment on our part.

The full ordinance, however, involves both a physical and a spiritual component. We accept the covenant through the physical portion of the ordinance. We must then live up to the terms of the covenant. God accepts our effort by providing the spiritual portion. For example, following our sincere repentance and baptism of water, He promises to provide a baptism of fire and of the Holy Ghost. Receiving the full ordinance requires both the baptism of water and the baptism of fire and the Holy Ghost. The sacrament, likewise, involves the physical action of partaking of bread and water by which we witness that we have complied with the requirements of the covenant. If that is the case, the Lord promises to fill us with His Spirit (the spiritual component of the ordinance). The ordinances of the temple are also comprised of a physical and a spiritual component. The physical components are readily discernable at the temple. You will have to look for their spiritual counterparts.

The physical parts of ordinances are also symbolic. God designed them the way He did in order to teach us something. "The Universe is built upon symbols . . . lifting our thoughts from man to God, from earth to heaven, from time to eternity. . . . God teaches with symbols; it is His favorite method of teaching."[18] There are many reasons why the Lord uses symbols to teach us. You can probably think of several. The greater our understanding of the symbolic teaching contained in an ordinance, the greater will be our respect and appreciation for it.

As an example, consider again the ordinance of baptism. Besides the obvious symbolism of being washed and cleansed from our sins, what are some of the other meanings associated with baptism? Here are four possibilities:

1. Baptism is a symbol of new birth or being born again (see John 3:3–7). At your physical birth there was water (amniotic fluid), blood (shed by your biological mother), and spirit (yours entering your body). In like manner, at your spiritual birth (or rebirth) there is once again water (baptismal), blood (shed by Christ in the Atonement), and spirit (that of the Holy Ghost) (see Moses 6:59). These same elements are present in both births. The baptismal font becomes a symbol of the womb and coming forth as a new child in Christ.

2. In addition, baptism is also a symbol of Christ's burial and resurrection. During immersion, we are placed below the water, in the same way the dead are buried below the ground. While immersed (and while dead), the breath of life is cut off. Breath (or life) is again restored as we come forth out of the water (or grave). In this sense, the font becomes a symbol of the grave and the baptism becomes a symbol of new life as the body and spirit are reunited

and come forth together from the grave in the resurrection (see Romans 6:3–6).

3. Baptism also symbolizes the death of the old "man" of sin, and the beginning of a new life in Christ (see Romans 6:4). The darkness of the watery grave (our former life) is left behind as we reopen our eyes into the light of the gospel (and a new life in Christ). Wendy Ulrich has taught; "[Baptism] reminds us [that] some part of us may have to die before we can claim new birth. False identities we have clung to, false traditions of our families or cultures, and false patterns we have copied must be dismantled and buried before new life can take hold."[19]

4. Finally, baptism points forward to our own eventual death and resurrection. We enact these events ceremonially through baptism before we experience them in reality. In this sense, the ordinance is not the final, real event, but instead points toward it. Baptism is the gate. It is the entrance to the path. But baptism also symbolically points to the end of that path which will include our own death and eventual resurrection.

Temple fonts are located below ground level to reinforce these symbols of the grave (see D&C 128:13). Placing the font on the backs of twelve oxen (just as in Solomon's temple) is symbolic of the twelve tribes of Israel. It is a reminder of the covenant status of the House of Israel and of adoption into it through the ordinances of baptism and of receiving the gift of the Holy Ghost. The oxen are often grouped in threes and face north, south, east, and west, reminding us of the scattering and subsequent gathering of the House of Israel from the four corners of the earth. The font on the back of the oxen is another reminder that the House of Israel is to carry these blessings to the rest of the world.

Living waters are symbolic of our Savior and the cleansing power of His Atonement. The baptizer who immerses and then brings the baptized person out of the water represents the Lord who holds the keys of death and resurrection. It is another reminder of our subjection to and total dependence upon Him. These symbols associated with baptism are designed by the Lord to teach us eternal truths. The ordinances embody eternal realities in a ceremonial act.

The end purpose of the gospel ordinances and their associated covenants is to prepare us to be able to eventually receive in reality the blessing and promises which we experience ceremonially through the ordinance. In this sense, the ordinances are a *spiritual creation*, which comes before a *physical creation* (see Moses 3:5). In other words, the ordinances become a blueprint, a map, or a Liahona for our lives. This is particularly true of the ordinances of the temple.

When you go to the temple for the first time, the new ordinances you receive might seem unfamiliar and might even be a little bit strange. They are different from what you know and experience in your daily life. But, like baptism or the sacrament, they are nothing to be overly concerned about. Enjoy the wonderful, rich outpouring of the Spirit there and accept the ordinances in faith. Over time as you return to the temple again and again, you will begin to see and understand the beautiful meanings and teachings built into the temple ordinances.

THE HOLY GHOST

Returning to the doctrine of Christ, Nephi testified:

> Wherefore, my beloved brethren, I know that if ye shall follow the Son, with full purpose of heart, acting no hypocrisy and no deception before God, but with real intent, repenting of your sins, witnessing unto the Father that ye are willing to take upon you the name of Christ, by baptism—yea, by following your Lord and your Savior down into the water, according to his word, behold, then shall ye receive the Holy Ghost; yea, then cometh the baptism of fire and of the Holy Ghost; and then can ye speak with the tongue of angels, and shout praises unto the Holy One of Israel. (2 Nephi 31:13)

Of all of the things God could bless us with in following our sincere repentance and baptism, He offers the baptism of fire and the Holy Ghost. Have you ever wondered why? The Holy Ghost is the greatest blessing God can give us at that point in our journey home. The scriptures testify that through gospel ordinances, the power of godliness begins to flow into our lives (see D&C 84:20). The Holy Ghost is part of the *power of Godliness*. We cannot become holy without it. For a more detailed discussion of why this is referred to as the baptism of fire and the Holy Ghost, please see chapter 4 of *Understanding Your Endowment*. This is a critical topic to our salvation and is explored more fully there.

Receiving the Holy Ghost doesn't necessarily occur automatically at baptism. When you were confirmed, hands were placed upon your head and you were told to *receive* it. That implies a process that you have to participate in. You must first repent, sincerely desire to live your baptismal covenants, and seek to have the Holy Ghost in your life. One good way is through sincere prayer. "Pray always, and I will pour out my Spirit upon you, and great shall be your blessing" (D&C 19:38). Can we expect to receive the Holy Ghost if we have not paid attention to the prerequisites outlined in the scriptures, namely faith, repentance, and baptism? When was the last time you felt the Holy Ghost's influence in your life? How often do you feel it? If you are not regularly experiencing the Spirit's influence in your life, how could you better focus your life on this core doctrine of Christ?

The scriptures also suggest that we can receive the Holy Ghost in varying degrees. In Doctrine and Covenants section 109, we learn that one of the purposes of the temple is so that we can "grow up in [the Lord], and receive a fulness of the Holy Ghost" (D&C 109:15). What do you think it means to receive a fulness of the Holy Ghost? Why are the temple ordinances a part of that process? At a minimum, recognize that they can aid us in obtaining greater access to the Holy Ghost and its influence in our life and can help us along the way to become more and more familiar with how the Lord speaks to us. This is a process that takes time.

We often talk of the Holy Ghost's role as a comforter, but equally, and perhaps more important, the Holy Ghost is also a sanctifier. To sanctify means to make holy, to purify, and to free from sin. "Now this is the commandment: Repent, all ye ends of the earth, and come unto me and be baptized in my name, that *ye may be sanctified by the reception of the Holy Ghost*, that ye may stand spotless before me at the last day" (3 Nephi 27:20; emphasis added). We need the sanctifying and purifying influence of the Spirit in our lives daily.

The Holy Ghost is also a revelator and a teacher. Joseph Smith recorded that after he and Oliver Cowdery were baptized, the Holy Ghost fell upon them. Their minds were enlightened and the Holy Ghost began to open the scriptures to their understandings (Joseph Smith—History 1:73–74). Those "aha" moments you have while reading the scriptures are often the Holy Ghost helping you to see and understand things you haven't before.

The Holy Ghost is also a guide in our lives. Nephi testified, "if ye will enter in by the way, and receive the Holy Ghost, it will show unto you all things what ye should do" (2 Nephi 32:5). What does "all things" include? If you stop and think about that for a minute, it's a pretty big promise. The

Lord is concerned with the details of your life. The decisions and choices you make matter. How can you make the many critical decisions you will face over the next ten years without help from the Lord? Without His guidance, how can you know if your life is on the course the Lord would have you take? And according to the *Lectures on Faith*, this is one of the three things you must have in order to have faith. One of the greatest skills you can develop in your life is learning to listen to and hear the Spirit. If there were any one thing I could give you, it would be to have a strong testimony of Christ and to have the Holy Ghost and personal revelation in your life.

In fact, the real effort required behind the doctrine of Christ is learning to receive and follow personal revelation in our lives. That allows us to keep the commandments He has given us. Most of the individual direction we receive will come through the Holy Ghost. "Behold, I will tell you in your mind and in your heart, by the Holy Ghost, which shall come upon you and which shall dwell in your heart. Now, behold, this is the spirit of revelation; behold, this is the spirit by which Moses brought the children of Israel through the Red Sea on dry ground" (D&C 8:2–3). Despite having stood in the Lord's presence and received instruction directly from Him, most of the instruction Moses received came through the still, small voice. It is the same for us. We may receive great spiritual manifestations through dreams, visions, angels, or other manifestations from the Lord. Don't disbelieve those things. But even if we receive those greater things, most of the direction and revelation from the Lord is going to come as quiet whispers to our soul. Learn to recognize and heed those promptings.

How do we learn to recognize the voice of the spirit in our lives? Elder Boyd K. Packer gave a wonderful talk, "The Candle of the Lord," on this very subject. In it, he described an experience he had trying to explain what the Spirit was like to a man who didn't believe in God. He related the following incident:

> I sat on a plane next to a professed atheist who pressed his disbelief in God so urgently that I bore my testimony to him. "You are wrong," I said, "there is a God. I *know* He lives!"
>
> He protested, "You don't *know*. Nobody *knows* that! You can't *know* it!" When I would not yield, the atheist, who was an attorney, asked perhaps the ultimate question on the subject of testimony. "All right," he said in a sneering, condescending way, "you say you know. Tell me *how* you know." . . .

When I used the words *Spirit* and *witness*, the atheist responded, "I don't know what you are talking about." The words *prayer*, *discernment*, and *faith*, were equally meaningless to him. "You see," he said, "you don't really know. If you did, you would be able to tell me *how you know*."

I felt, perhaps, that I had borne my testimony to him unwisely and was at a loss as to what to do. Then came the experience! Something came into my mind. And I mention here a statement of the Prophet Joseph Smith: "A person may profit by noticing the first intimation of the spirit of revelation; for instance, when you feel pure intelligence flowing into you, it may give you sudden strokes of ideas . . . and thus by learning the Spirit of God and understanding it, you may grow into the principle of revelation, until you become perfect in Christ Jesus."[20]

Such an idea came into my mind and I said to the atheist, "Let me ask if you know what salt tastes like."

"Of course I do," was his reply.

"When did you taste salt last?"

"I just had dinner on the plane."

"You just think you know what salt tastes like," I said.

He insisted, "I know what salt tastes like as well as I know anything."

"If I gave you a cup of salt and a cup of sugar and let you taste them both, could you tell the salt from the sugar?"

"Now you are getting juvenile," was his reply. "Of course I could tell the difference. I know what salt tastes like. It is an everyday experience—I know it as well as I know anything."

"Then," I said, "assuming that I have never tasted salt, explain to me just what it tastes like."

After some thought, he ventured, "Well-I-uh, it is not sweet and it is not sour."

"You've told me what it isn't, not what it is."

After several attempts, of course, he could not do it. He could not convey, in words alone, so ordinary an experience as tasting salt. I bore testimony to him once again and said, "I know there is a God. You ridiculed that testimony and said that if I *did* know, I would be able to tell you exactly *how* I know. My friend, spiritually speaking, I have tasted salt. I am no more able to convey to you in words how this knowledge has come than you are to tell me what salt tastes like. But I say to you again, there is a God! He does live! And just because you don't know, don't try to tell me that I don't know, for I do!"

As we parted, I heard him mutter, "I don't need your religion for a crutch! I don't need it."

From that experience forward, I have never been embarrassed or ashamed that I could not explain in words alone everything I know spiritually.[21]

Sometimes the Spirit's voice and direction is unmistakable. Generally, however, it is quiet, and we must be still and learn to listen to it. It can be difficult to describe. Elder Packer continues:

> The voice of the Spirit is described in the scripture as being neither "loud" nor "harsh." It is "not a voice of thunder, neither . . . voice of a great tumultuous noise." But rather, "a still voice of perfect mildness, as if it had been a whisper," and it can "pierce even to the very soul" and "cause [the heart] to burn." (3 Nephi 11:3; Helaman 5:30; D&C 85:6–7.) Remember, Elijah found the voice of the Lord was not in the wind, nor in the earthquake, nor in the fire, but was a "still small voice" (1 Kings 19:12).
>
> The Spirit does not get our attention by shouting or shaking us with a heavy hand. Rather it whispers. It caresses so gently that if we are preoccupied we may not feel it at all. . . .
>
> Occasionally it will press just firmly enough for us to pay heed. But most of the time, if we do not heed the gentle feeling, the Spirit will withdraw and wait until we come seeking and listening and say in our manner and expression, like Samuel of ancient times, "Speak [Lord], for thy servant heareth" (1 Samuel 3:10).[22]

Recognizing the Spirit is something we all must learn and experience for ourselves. It probably varies somewhat from person to person. Almost like learning a foreign language, our ability can grow and expand over time as we pay attention to that which we receive from the Lord. If you seek it, and if you follow the prerequisite steps with full purpose of heart, you will receive the Holy Ghost. You will recognize it when you do. To some extent, the degree to which we have the Spirit's influence in our life depends upon our diligence.

Our initial experiences often begin very small and humbly. It may even require some faith to recognize and accept that a feeling or an idea came as an answer from the Lord in response to our petition. However, as we act upon these whisperings, we come to see and understand additional truth (see Alma 32:28). Then follows confirmation that the promptings were of God. As we nurture the influence of the Holy Spirit in our lives, our ability to recognize promptings increases. If we stay on this path, the frequency of these communications from God increases in our lives and we begin to grow up in the Lord.

Nephi's experience is instructive. His first recorded experience with the Holy Ghost was simply feelings that softened his heart and allowed him to believe (see 1 Nephi 2:16). Later, he was able to hear the voice of the Lord in the quiet promptings he received. This voice of the Lord comes most often to our minds. We may be given an answer or taught something we have never thought of before. The voice communicates information and words; it is more than just a feeling from God. It is another level in our ability to communicate with the Lord.

After being true to the promptings he received and after further spiritual growth, Nephi eventually saw visions, entertained angels, and was ministered to by the Savior. These kinds of exceptional spiritual experiences do occur. They are real. But as a general rule, we don't experience them until after we have learned to recognize and follow the voice of the Spirit in our lives.

In addition to giving answers and information, the Spirit often provides direction or service the Lord would have us do. In my experience, these promptings are usually for something we are not planning to do and may not even want to do. If you think about it, this only makes sense. If we were going to do something anyway in the normal course of our life, the Spirit would have no need to prompt us. Perhaps this is why it is often so easy to ignore or argue with the promptings we receive. They require us to interrupt our plans or what we are doing. Understanding this, however, may also help us to better recognize and respond to these promptings, especially when they are subtle.

Jules Allred shared this beautiful insight: "If God wants to communicate with us, He will do so by connecting spiritually with those portions of us that are most like HIM; He will persuade us using love, light, peace, joy, and by the pure intelligence that is communicated by the Holy Ghost. If Satan wants to communicate with us, he will do so by connecting with those portions of us that are most like HIM; he will persuade us using fear, confusion, doubt, insecurity, irrationality, etc. In other words, for God or Satan to communicate with us, we have to be partly LIKE them. If you overcome the parts of YOURSELF that are most like Satan, he will be less able to connect and communicate with you. If you strengthen the parts of yourself that are most like God, you will be more able to connect with and communicate with Him."[23]

If there is anything you gain from this book, I sincerely hope and pray it will be a desire to have the Spirit in your life more often and in greater measure. Learn to recognize the Lord's voice to you. Follow His direction and promptings in your life. I testify that you can and that it will get easier over time. The Lord wants to talk with you; He loves you and will give you direction in your life. He will lead and guide you, if you will seek it. The Lord also wants to teach you. He is more talkative than I ever would have believed when I was younger. Speak with Him daily.

HOMEWORK

1. Start a spiritual journal. Keep it separate from your daily journal, kind of like Nephi's small and large plates. Record in your spiritual journal impressions and thoughts from the Spirit, answers to prayers, and insights gained from your study. Don't write this for anyone else or worry about anyone else reading it. Just pour your heart and raw feelings into it. It is just for you, no one else. You will find that it is helpful to look back through this as the years pass to see your growth and to see the Lord's hand in your life. Record His promises to you and how they are later fulfilled.

2. How does the Lord communicate with you? Take time to ponder about some of the answers you have received from Him. Thoughts can be our own, from the Lord, or suggestions from the adversary. Learn to recognize and distinguish the source of these "voices" in your mind. Reread the quote from Jules Allred. What could you do to improve your communication with the Lord? If you're not hearing the spirit's voice in your life, you may want to pray for ears to hear and eyes to see. Ask for the gift of discernment to be able to distinguish the Spirit's promptings from your own thoughts.

3. Consider the promises contained in these two scriptures and what they can mean in your life: "If thou shalt ask, thou shalt receive revelation upon revelation, knowledge upon knowledge, that thou mayest know the mysteries and peaceable things—that which bringeth joy, that which bringeth life eternal" (D&C 42:61). "The Spirit shall be given unto you by the prayer of faith" (D&C 42:14).

4. When you attend the temple, pay attention to what the endowment teaches about gaining revelation from the Lord.

Chapter 6
ENDURING TO THE END

Some people laughed openly. Others tried to hide their sneers. Many were concerned. The old man might kill himself. He couldn't actually be serious, could he? No one knew quite what to think. The runners assembled at the starting line were young, world-class athletes who had come to test the limits of their endurance. They were about to begin a grueling ultramarathon—a 544-mile run from Sydney to Melbourne, Australia. All had trained very hard for the event.

And so when Cliff Young, age sixty-one, showed up to the starting line, no one took him seriously. He was much too old for such a physical feat. Cliff was told, "You're crazy. There is no way you can finish this race." His response was simply, "Yes, I can. I grew up on a farm where we couldn't afford horses or tractors, and the whole time I was growing up, whenever the storms would roll in, I'd have to go out and round up the sheep. We had two thousand sheep on two thousand acres. Sometimes I would have to run those sheep for two or three days. It took a long time, but I'd always catch them."[24]

As the race started, Cliff was quickly left behind by the pros. Some teased him because he didn't even run properly. Cliff shuffled along in an awkward gait. All day long the runners pressed on before stopping for about six hours of sleep. When dawn came on the second day, everyone woke to a surprise. Not only was Cliff still in the race, he had continued jogging all through the night without sleeping, and by morning he had overtaken some of the runners.

The next day and the next, the scene repeated. Each night he continued to run while the others slept, gradually moving up the ranks of the runners. Cliff ended up finishing the race in five days, fifteen hours, and four minutes. Not only did he win, but he beat the prior course record by two full days. It was a real-life tortoise and hare story.

When Cliff was awarded the winning prize of ten thousand dollars, he gave it away to some of the other runners whom he had met and felt needed it more than he did. He hadn't known there was a prize and said he just wanted to see if he could do it. Today, the "Young Shuffle" has been recognized as very efficient, using less energy than a more traditional gait. Many ultra-marathon runners have adopted it. Furthermore, competitors since Cliff often do not sleep. Winning the race requires runners to go all night as well as all day, just as Cliff Young first did.

There is a good moral in Cliff's story for each of us. When it comes to eternal life, the race is not won by the swift or the most talented, but by those who persevere. "Wherefore . . . let us lay aside every weight, and the sin which doth so easily beset us, and let us run with patience the race that is set before us" (Hebrews 12:1).

THE RACE OF LIFE

The doctrine of Christ includes the principle of enduring to the end. Nephi testified, "wherefore, ye must press forward with a steadfastness in Christ, having a perfect brightness of hope, and a love of God and of all men. Wherefore, if ye shall press forward, feasting upon the word of Christ, and *endure to the end*, behold, thus saith the Father: Ye shall have eternal life." (2 Nephi 31:20; emphasis added).

The first principles of faith and repentance are accompanied by the first ordinances of baptism and the laying on of hands for the gift of the Holy Ghost. It follows then that the ordinances of the temple are the ordinances of enduring to the end. They are associated with our spiritual growth and maturation.

The Lord knows the road, what we are capable of, and what we need along the way. We don't need to run faster than we have strength, but we do need to be diligent (see Mosiah 4:27). In our journey back, we encounter several potential obstacles including apathy, deception, trials, and sin. These are some of the primary enemies to endurance. We'll look at each of these quickly and see how the Holy Ghost and the temple can provide the solution to each.

APATHY

To be apathetic means to lack enthusiasm for or an interest in something, in this case, Christ and His gospel. Our lives are very busy. It is easy for other cares to crowd out the things of the Spirit. We can lose focus and find ourselves going through the motions without really being anxiously engaged. Think about the Zoramites with their Rameumptom. They attended church each week and then returned to their homes and never spoke of their God again until the next Sabbath (see Alma 31:23). It is easy to scoff at them from a distance, but do we sometimes fall into the same error? There certainly have been times in my life when I have been too distracted by the cares of the world. Amulek likewise testified that the Spirit often called him but he refused to listen (see Alma 10:6). He was too busy with all of the day-to-day things that he was pursuing and was ignoring the things God wanted him to do.

Nephi warns us against several specific pitfalls that can contribute to or be related to apathy: one was the notion that all is well in Zion. Thus lulled to sleep, Nephi tells us of the awful result: "and thus the devil cheateth their souls, and leadeth them away carefully down to hell" (2 Nephi 28:21). Can you imagine the regret and remorse we would feel upon returning to the Lord, knowing how very much of His truth we have been given, and yet allowing ourselves to get so caught up in the things of this world that we neglected to really find and do His will in our lives?

Another related pitfall is our tendency to want to "eat, drink, and be merry" (2 Nephi 28:7). Like a river, it is easy for us to take the path of least resistance through life. This, however, can cheat our souls of the very growth and preparation we came down here to receive, if we put off the day of our repentance and do not use this life to prepare to meet God (see Alma 12:24). Nephi again records the awful consequence: "they are grasped with death, and hell; and death, and hell, and the devil, and all that have been seized therewith must stand before the throne of God, and be judged according to their works, from whence they must go into the place prepared for them, even a lake of fire and brimstone, which is endless torment. Therefore, wo be unto him that is at ease in Zion! Wo be unto him that crieth: All is well!" (2 Nephi 28:23–25).

Lehi pled with his sons to arise from the dust and be men, begging them to "Awake, my sons; put on the armor of righteousness. Shake off the chains with which ye are bound, and come forth out of obscurity, and arise from the dust" (2 Nephi 1:23). Apathy is being asleep and in the dust. We may not even be aware of it and, like Laman and Lemuel, may need a stern warning and rebuke from a loving parent or friend. Their scriptural warnings are recorded for our benefit as well.

In contrast to these sobering warnings, Christ testifies that He is standing at the door of our lives, knocking. "Behold, I stand at the door, and knock: if any man hear my voice, and open the door, I will come in to him, and will sup with him, and he with me. To him that overcometh will I grant to sit with me in my throne, even as I also overcame, and am set down with my Father in his throne" (Revelation 3:20–21). This knocking occurs mostly through the Holy Ghost—but it is up to us to open the door and let Him in our lives. The choice is ours.

In our modern world, one of the easiest ways Satan can get us off course is to simply get our lives so filled with video games, friends, Facebook, movies, music, books, sports, work, school, or other activities that we neglect our spiritual growth and development. There are so many distractions surrounding us constantly. These things can become addictive and eat up too much of our time, and some of them are spiritually damaging. Have courage to put them in their proper place or even to set them aside and seek for better things.

Of course, life needs to have a balance. And I am not campaigning against video games or anything else here. We simply need to keep all good things in their proper place and time. Sometimes that is difficult, as it's easy to get out of balance. We can't neglect our schooling, work, or family responsibilities, but our focus first and foremost should continually be on the Lord. As President Benson taught, "When we put God first, all other things fall into their proper place or drop out of our lives."[25] Attending the temple regularly provides us with a wonderful opportunity to step out of the world for a time and to take an inventory of our lives. The endowment can help us to put God first by reminding us of those things that truly matter.

DECEPTION

Deception is another obstacle. This one is a problem for each of us to some degree. To be deceived is to believe that something is true when it is not. That makes recognizing deception very difficult, especially when those false things we believe are wired into us at an early age through our traditions and culture. The scriptures testify that Satan deceives the entire world (see Revelation 12:9). His lies are found everywhere. We all have false ideas about ourselves, others, and even God and His work. The Book of Mormon refers to this problem of deception as unbelief. We move from *unbelief* to *belief* as we accept truth and give up old notions that are false. Without this process, we may end up "dwindling in unbelief," off course, and unaware.

How do we obtain truth and set aside our unbelief? Spend time studying and pondering the scriptures, which are the standard against which all truth should be measured. Take your questions to God to get answers. Once again the Holy Ghost is also a critical part of the solution. We are promised that by it we "may know the truth of all things" (Moroni 10:5). Most of our answers from God and most of the revelation we receive will come through the Holy Ghost. Our lives must be filled with a relentless pursuit for truth, for only the truth can set us free (see John 8:32). The Holy Ghost is indispensable to us in discerning truth from error.

Alma summarized the process. As you read this scripture, think of hardening your heart as rejecting or arguing with the Spirit's promptings to you instead of yielding your heart to its influence and following it.

> He that will harden his heart, the same receiveth the lesser portion of the word; and he that will not harden his heart, to him is given the greater portion of the word, until it is given unto him to know the mysteries of God until he know them in full.
>
> And they that will harden their hearts, to them is given the lesser portion of the word until they know nothing concerning his mysteries; and then they are taken captive by the devil, and led by his will down to destruction. Now this is what is meant by the chains of hell. (Alma 12:10–11)

God freely gives to all His children, but how much we receive from Him is largely up to us. We regulate it by our heed and diligence (see Alma 12:9). No matter how much we gain, we must remain humble and teachable. The temple endowment testifies that each of us needs to seek further light and knowledge from the Lord and from His messengers.

Sometimes we reach a plateau where we stop growing or become content with what we have received from the Lord and stop seeking more. Nephi warned us specifically in our day against this. He taught:

> Wo be unto him that shall say: We have received the word of God, and we need no more of the word of God, for we have enough! For behold,

thus saith the Lord God: I will give unto the children of men line upon line, precept upon precept, here a little and there a little; and blessed are those who hearken unto my precepts, and lend an ear unto my counsel, for they shall learn wisdom; for unto him that receiveth I will give more; and from them that shall say, We have enough, from them shall be taken away even that which they have. (2 Nephi 28:29–30)

If this describes us, we will eventually come to regret our course and wasted opportunity. We will feel the "wo" Nephi warns of.

On the other hand, the scriptures also teach that "if a person gains more knowledge and intelligence in this life through his diligence and obedience than another, he will have so much the advantage in the world to come" (D&C 130:19). Abraham testified that he had been "a follower of righteousness, desiring also to be one who possessed great knowledge, and to be a greater follower of righteousness, and to possess a greater knowledge" (Abraham 1:2). This is a wonderful example for us to follow.

Some years ago, I found myself on a plateau where my spiritual growth and learning had stopped. At the time, I was attending the temple weekly and living a good life. I felt that I had received enough and simply needed to "endure to the end." Fortunately, the Lord knew how very much I lacked (and still do) and brought some things to my attention that started to bring additional growth and learning into my life. Since that day, my understanding of the gospel has grown immensely, maybe doubled or tripled from what it was back then. And yet there is still more. The Lord told me the other day that I have much to learn. That is so true, and I look forward to continuing in this journey. The old adage that "the teacher will appear when the student is ready" seems true when it comes to the gospel. Recognize there is more for each of us to learn. Prepare yourself. Ask, seek, and knock, as the scriptures repeatedly testify and the endowment affirms: the Lord will answer (see, for example, Matthew 7:7, 3 Nephi 14:7, D&C 88:63).

In a future, millennial day, truth will be commonplace and will cover the earth. "Wherefore, all things which have been revealed unto the children of men shall at that day be revealed; and Satan shall have power over the hearts of the children of men no more" (2 Nephi 30:18). In the face of this ocean of truth, Satan's lies will have no more power. He will be "cast out" because he can no longer deceive.

We needn't wait—in fact, we cannot wait for that future millennial day. This can happen for us individually much sooner. As we gather enough truth and light and conform our lives to it, Satan's influence over us gradually ends. We can join the ranks of those who are sanctified enough that they can only look upon sin with abhorrence. It has no power over their hearts and no appeal to them.

God has given us three great tools to avoid being deceived. The first is the scriptures. They are part of the iron rod against which all else should be measured. If we hearken and hold fast to the word of God, we will not be blinded or overcome. Consider this promise: "whoso would hearken [*hearken* means to listen and obey] unto the word of God, and would hold fast unto it, they would never perish; neither could the temptations and the fiery darts of the adversary overpower them unto blindness, to lead them away to destruction" (1 Nephi 15:24). Notice that blindness, or being deceived, eventually leads to destruction. This is why deception is such a problem.

The second tool to avoid deception is our temple covenants. President David O. McKay defined the endowment as the "truest philosophy of life ever given to man."[26] It stands in stark contrast to the philosophies of men mingled with scripture that we find in the world around us.

And the third part of the rod is the Holy Ghost. By its power we "may know the truth of all things" (Moroni 10:5). Anything that contradicts the scriptures, the temple covenants, and the Holy Ghost is not a true message, regardless of its source.

TRIALS

Trials are another obstacle to endurance. They can be difficult, sometimes more so than we ever thought possible. But trials, like our weaknesses, can be a great blessing to us *if* we allow them to bring us closer to our Savior. Once again, the choice is ours. We can *turn to* or *away from* God during times of trial. Some question God's justice and turn from Him. Others allow their trials to bring them closer to their Savior even to the point that they can experience great joy and peace even in the midst of their suffering. We see an example of both responses in the Book of Mormon: "But behold, because of the exceedingly great length of the war between the Nephites and the Lamanites many had become hardened, because of the exceedingly great length of the war; and many were softened because of their afflictions, insomuch that they did humble themselves before God, even in the depth of humility" (Alma 62:41).

And in another place, the Nephites were again suffering through affliction, "nevertheless they did fast and pray oft, and did wax stronger and stronger in their humility, and firmer and firmer in the faith of Christ, unto the filling their souls with joy and consolation, yea, even to the purifying and the sanctification of their hearts, which sanctification cometh because of their yielding their hearts unto God" (Helaman 3:35). This is our example. The Holy Ghost is our comforter during these times. We need not fear our own Gethsemane; whatever we are called to go through, God can turn it to our blessing.

Consider this promise: "And now, my brethren, I desire that ye shall plant this word in your hearts, and as it beginneth to swell even so nourish it by your faith. And behold, it will become a tree, springing up in you unto everlasting life. *And then may God grant unto you that your burdens may be light, through the joy of his Son.* And even all this can ye do if ye will" (Alma 33:23; emphasis added). He truly can make our burdens light, and, at times, even turn them into joy.

Christ understands our suffering perfectly. When Joseph Smith cried out in anguish from the depths of his soul in the Liberty Jail, the Lord gave him peace, reminded him that his afflictions wouldn't last, and told him to endure them well (see D&C 121:7–8). And then, to comfort Joseph further, He lists some of the things Joseph has had to endure, including this poignant scene: "If with a drawn sword thine enemies tear thee from the bosom of thy wife, and of thine offspring, and thine elder son, although but six years of age, shall cling to thy garments, and shall say, My father, my father, why can't you stay with us? O, my father, what are the men going to do with you?" (D&C 122:6). Christ is patiently and lovingly letting Joseph know that He is aware of every small detail of Joseph's sufferings. It is the same for us. We don't go through our trials alone. He then reassured Joseph, "know thou, my son, that all these things shall give thee experience, and shall be for thy good" (D&C 122:7). Christ patiently reminds Joseph that He has descended below all things (see D&C 122:8). Are any greater than He?

Sometimes people have the mistaken idea that living the gospel allows us to avoid the trials and problems of life. Part of that misunderstanding may stem from scriptures that promise if we keep the commandments we shall prosper in the land (see 2 Nephi 1:20, for example). These types of promises are sometimes misconstrued into a *gospel of success* mentality. It is the belief that the more *righteous* I am, the more success, money, happiness, and so on that I will experience in life. But that's a false premise and not what the scripture means. To prosper is to fulfill and succeed in our life's mission; it is not a promise of life on easy street. It is true that to some extent the commandments do protect us from unwanted consequences. But all of us are going to encounter difficulty, opposition, and trials in our lives. Even righteous Nephi, who testified that he was highly favored of the Lord, also testified that he had seen many afflictions in his days (see 1 Nephi 1:1).

Why is this adversity necessary? Trials serve an important purpose in our growth and development. We see an example of why this is so in nature. Both diamonds and coal are formed from carbon. Diamonds require just the right combination of heat, pressure, and time in order to form. Trials help provide the same conditions for us. They are a necessary part of putting off the natural man (coal) and becoming a saint (diamond). If in the furnace of affliction we allow our trials to cause us to question God's justice or His love and mercy, rather than turning to Him for strength and comfort, then our trials may become stumbling blocks rather than blessings.

At some point we all find ourselves in the ashes of life. We may arrive there from our own mistakes and sins or through no fault of our own. Regardless, we all must pass through our own Gethsemane. Turn to the Lord in those times of trial. Let them bring you closer to Him. Let the Holy Ghost comfort and sustain you during those times and recognize that part of Christ's ministry is to eventually give you "beauty for ashes, the oil of joy for mourning, the garment of praise for the spirit of heaviness" (Isaiah 61:3). Truly He can consecrate all of our afflictions for our gain (see 2 Nephi 2:2). As a result of your trials, you may grow closer to the Lord than you could have without them. The temple can be a wonderful refuge during these storms. Within its walls many find the strength to continue forward. In the end, with greater perspective, we can recognize our trials to be among the greatest blessings the Lord can give us.

Sin and Temptation

Sin can also be an obstacle to our endurance, through discouragement or losing the Spirit. The mists of darkness in Lehi's dream were the temptations of the devil that caused people to let go of the rod and lose their way (see 1 Nephi 12:17). The scriptures testify that when we try to cover up our sins (hiding or not acknowledging our mistakes), gratify our pride (seeking to build ourselves up in others' eyes or appear better than we are), follow our vain ambitions (seeking our own will rather than the Lord's will), or when we try to control or compel others, then the Spirit is grieved and departs from us (see D&C 121:37). Before we are aware of it, we are left on our own (see D&C 121:38)—and left to our own, we will fail. Satan stands by ever ready to step in.

God is patient with us and is quick to forgive our mistakes and sins. But we must repent and seek for His Spirit and His sanctifying influence. We do not become holy on our own; we need the influence of the Spirit in our lives daily. Seek to have it with you as often as you can.

In the process of time, eventually we can be sanctified to the point that we lose all desire to sin. "Now they, after being sanctified by the Holy Ghost, having their garments made white, being pure and spotless before God, could not look upon sin save it were with abhorrence; and there were many, exceedingly great many, who were made pure and entered into the rest of the Lord their God" (Alma 13:12). Christ would like to bring us to this same state as well, and He will if we let Him. He will do so by leading us through the Spirit. It's yet another reason that we must learn to recognize and follow His voice in our lives.

Eventually, the Holy Ghost can become our constant companion (see D&C 121:46), but it does not start out that way. Initially, we receive bits and pieces—here a little and there a little. King Benjamin called these moments the "enticings of the Holy Spirit" and taught that we need to "yield" to them (see Mosiah 3:19). Yielding includes accepting them, acting on them, and also remembering them. God respects our agency and always allows us to accept or reject. We can have a hard heart or a soft one.

For example, we might feel the Spirit very strongly during a testimony meeting or at a fireside or during the sacrament. There have been some Sundays when I was filled with the Spirit throughout the day, but then the next morning I woke to find it was gone. On other occasions, I have been so filled at the temple that the spiritual afterglow lasted for days. These spiritual experiences we have are real, but they eventually fade and we are left to muddle forward on our own. It is at that point that we have a choice. We either accept or reject the experience. We can choose to remember it and hold onto it, or we can question if it was real or not. Satan steps in to tempt us and to try us. He is allowed to have his influence.

Even the Savior was not exempt. Following His baptism and the opening of the heavens, He spent forty days in the wilderness to be with God (see JST Matthew 4:1). Following that rich spiritual communion with His father, "he was afterwards an hungered, and was left to be tempted of the devil" (JST Matthew 4:2). It was the same "when Moses was caught up into an exceedingly high mountain, and he saw God face to face, and he talked with him, and the glory of God was upon Moses; therefore Moses could endure his presence" (Moses 1:1–2). After God withdrew, Moses was "left unto himself" (Moses 1:9), and Satan stepped in, saying, "Moses, son of man, worship me" (Moses 1:12).

These were dramatic spiritual experiences and confrontations, but they reveal a pattern that is manifest along our spiritual journey home. We have outpourings of the Spirit in our lives and then are left unto ourselves to again be tempted and tried by Satan's influences. Lehi saw these mists of darkness that we must pass through. The key was in clinging to the iron rod—which includes not only the scriptures but also all of the spiritual experiences and directions that we have been given. Hold to and trust the word of the Lord and press forward through the darkness until the light reappears. Eventually the Holy Ghost returns and once again teaches, strengthens, and witnesses to our souls.

Once again, I repeat Jules Allred's insight: "If you overcome the parts of YOURSELF that are most like Satan, he will be less able to connect and communicate with you. If you strengthen the parts of yourself that are most like God, you will be more able to connect with and communicate with Him."[27] Sin dulls our receptivity to God's voice.

The Purpose of the Doctrine of Christ

Nephi concludes his remarks on this doctrine with a couple of questions and answers, providing some further clarifications about what to do after we are on the path. He counsels us to, "feast upon the words of Christ; for behold, the *words of Christ* will tell you all things what ye should do. . . . Again I say unto you that if ye will enter in by the way, and receive the Holy Ghost, it will show unto you all things what ye should do" (2 Nephi 32:3, 5; emphasis added). That is the challenge in front of us: to 1) enter in by the way, or in other words, get on the strait and narrow path and then, 2) follow what Christ tells and shows us to do thereafter.

We obtain the word of Christ primarily from four sources: through authorized gospel ordinances (including those in the temple), from the scriptures, by the mouths of angels,[28] and through the Holy Ghost (which would include the words of Christ given directly to you). The temple endowment testifies of our need to receive Christ's words from each of these sources. We must learn, ponder, and search the scriptures. We must hearken to God's messages delivered by His servants. And most of all, we must get personal revelation. Joseph Smith taught that "salvation cannot come without revelation."[29]

Our salvation is dependent upon getting and then following the words of Christ in our lives. A significant portion of this can only occur through personal revelation. In the beginning, this may start with our need to gain a personal testimony or witness concerning our Savior, God's love for us, the prophet Joseph Smith, the truth of the Book of Mormon, and so on, but the Spirit's influence in our lives must not end there. Each of us has different responsibilities and circumstances in our lives. We were sent to accomplish different missions and works for the Lord. We each are blessed with different gifts, talents, and abilities, but no matter our mission in life, the only way to succeed in our individual journey is to receive Christ's directions for us. We must receive personal revelation and follow it.

Prayer is critical to this entire process. It is foolish to think we can be saved without spending significant and meaningful time on our knees in prayer. Nephi testified that if we don't understand the Lord's words it is because "ye ask not, neither do ye knock; wherefore, ye are not brought into the light, but must perish in the dark" (2 Nephi 32:4). How many times do the scriptures admonish us to ask, seek, and knock? That is a key for each of us. To some extent, the Lord is bound until we do. Nephi testifies that we "must pray always" and "not perform any thing unto the Lord save in the first place ye shall pray unto the Father in the name of Christ, that he will consecrate thy performance unto thee, that thy performance may be for the welfare of thy soul" (2 Nephi 32:9).

With these ideas in mind, we might well ask, where is all of this leading us? What is the doctrine of Christ ultimately meant to bring about? Nephi answers: "Behold, this is the doctrine of Christ, and there will be no more doctrine given until after he shall manifest himself unto *you in the flesh*. And when he shall manifest himself unto you in the flesh, the things which he shall say unto you shall ye observe to do" (2 Nephi 32:6; emphasis added). Did you catch that? The doctrine of Christ is meant to bring you back into Christ's presence. This is another of the central messages of the Book of Mormon. It contains example after example of those who followed this doctrine back into Christ's presence. The Book of Mormon stands as a testimony and as an invitation for each of us to do the same.

Nephi has said all that he is permitted to say. He has told us these things as plainly as he can. He knows much more but "the Spirit stoppeth mine utterance" (2 Nephi 32:7). The rest we have to receive individually from Christ. Sadly, Nephi knows that many of us won't believe him. We don't believe it possible or that he really means what he says, and so Nephi records, "I am left to mourn because of the unbelief, and the wickedness, and the ignorance, and the stiffneckedness of men" (2 Nephi 32:7). It is up to us to fix these conditions in our own lives. The temple is designed to help us and is another witness of these things. Joseph Smith also testified of these things and summarized the doctrine of Christ as follows:

> After a person has faith in Christ, repents of his sins, and is baptized for the remission of his sins and receives the Holy Ghost, (by the laying on of hands), which is the first Comforter, then let him continue to humble himself before God, hungering and thirsting after righteousness, and living by every word of God, and the Lord will soon say unto him, Son, thou shalt be exalted. When the Lord has thoroughly proved him, and finds that the man is determined to serve Him at all hazards, then the man will find his calling and his election made sure, then it will be his privilege to receive the other Comforter. . . .
>
> Now what is this other Comforter? It is no more nor less than the Lord Jesus Christ Himself; and this is the sum and substance of the whole matter; that when any man obtains this last Comforter, he will have the personage of Jesus Christ to attend him, or appear unto him from time to time, and even He will manifest the Father unto him, and they will take up their abode with him, and the visions of the heavens will be opened unto him, and the Lord will teach him face to face, and he may have a perfect knowledge of the mysteries of the Kingdom of God.[30]

This doctrine is so foundational to the gospel that Joseph also taught, "It is the first principle of the Gospel to know for a certainty the Character of God, and to know that we may converse with him as one man converses with another."[31]

Because of the Fall, mankind is shut out of God's presence. God wants us to return. The only way back is to repent and call upon God in the name of His Son. The path is outlined in the doctrine of Christ and further expounded in the temple endowment. If we live it, we will receive mercy, be redeemed, and enter into the rest of the Lord. To be redeemed means to be brought back into the presence of God (see Ether 3:13–14). The scriptures often call this "entering into the rest of the Lord" (see Alma 60:13, Moroni 7:3) and, as they testify over and over, this can happen here in mortality (see, for example, Alma 12:33–35). The temple endowment testifies of and is given to prepare us for these blessings.

Years ago, Elder Melvin J. Ballard shared such an experience in our day. He wrote:

> I recall an experience which I had two years ago, bearing witness to my soul of the reality of His death, of His crucifixion, and His resurrection, that I shall never forget. I bear it to you tonight, to you, young boys and girls; not with a spirit to glory over it, but with a grateful heart and with thanksgiving in my soul. I know that He lives, and I know that through Him men must find their salvation. . . .
>
> Away on the Fort Peck Reservation where I was doing missionary work with some of our brethren, laboring among the Indians, seeking the Lord for light to decide certain matters pertaining to our work there . . . I found myself one evening in the dreams of the night in that sacred building, the temple. After a season of prayer and rejoicing I was informed that I should have the privilege of entering into one of those rooms to meet a glorious Personage, and, as I entered the door, I saw, seated on a raised platform, the most glorious Being my eyes have ever beheld or that I ever conceived existed in all the eternal worlds. As I approached to be introduced, he arose and stepped towards me with extended arms, and he smiled as he softly spoke my name. If I shall live to be a million years old, I shall never forget that smile. He took me into his arms and kissed me, pressed me to his bosom, and blessed me, until the marrow of my bones seemed to melt! When he had finished, I fell at his feet, and, as I bathed them with my tears and kisses, I saw the prints of the nails in the feet of the Redeemer of the world. The feeling that I had in the presence of Him who hath all things in His hands, to have His love, His affection, and His blessing was such that if I ever can receive that of which I had but a foretaste, I would give all that I am, all that I ever hope to be to feel what I then felt!
>
> Go to the sacrament table. Ah, that is a blessed privilege that I now rejoice in, and I would be ashamed, I know, as I felt then, to stand in His presence and try to offer any apology or any excuse for not having kept His commandments and honored Him by bearing witness, before the Father and before men, that I believe in Him, and that I take upon me His blessed name, and that I live by and through Him spiritually.[32]

CHAPTER 6

HOMEWORK

1. How might you more fully accept and live the doctrine of Christ in your life?
2. How does the sacrament fit in with this doctrine?
3. When did you last feel the Spirit in your life? What could you do to have it with you more often?

Part 2

YOUR TEMPLE EXPERIENCE

INTRODUCTION

Why do we have additional ordinances beyond baptism and the sacrament as part of the gospel? In light of our discussion of the doctrine of Christ in part 1, why do we also need the temple? How does it all tie together? What will my own temple experience be like? What commitments will be required of me? We will discuss answers to these questions in part 2.

The roots of the endowment are ancient, stretching back to Adam and Eve as they received their endowments directly from God. From our first parents, these things were passed down from generation to generation before eventually becoming lost and obscured. Even then, traces of these rituals remain scattered throughout history among many peoples and civilizations. Joseph Smith restored these things as part of the latter-day dispensation.

The endowment presentation teaches the plan of salvation through ceremony and symbolism. It is presented as a drama through the figurative persons of Adam and Eve, and they are representative of each of us. The endowment truly is a model of your own life including your premortal life, your physical birth, and your individual fall through sin symbolized by the tree of knowledge. Through symbols, it then outlines the steps in your spiritual rebirth and your journey back to God's presence. It points to your obligation in mortality to seek for further light, knowledge, and experience which God will send to aid you. It lays out the path which Christ followed, and which you must also follow as His disciple, and places you under covenant to do so. You are taught to pray in a manner so as to be able to receive answers from the Lord. And finally, the endowment presentation culminates at the veil (symbolic of the tree of life) where you are prepared to communicate with the Lord and then to eventually return to His presence.

All of this is done through symbolism and ritual. Your endowment essentially gives you a map or a blueprint or a Liahona. It is extremely valuable, but it is not complete until you come to understand what is being taught and then implement it in your actual, daily life. You must apply and live the teachings in order to receive the blessings you seek. This takes time. Ultimately your endowment is between you and God. He alone is the "keeper of the gate" (2 Nephi 9:41). It is from Him that you may receive the blessings outlined in the temple. The endowment is given to show you how to obtain them.

There are three primary purposes for our temple endowment. One is to testify of Christ. The second is to complete our spiritual rebirth and help us grow into spiritual maturity. And the third is to bring us unto Christ to be redeemed by Him. The temple centers around our relationship with our Savior, and, like the law of Moses anciently, the temple ceremonies serve as a schoolmaster in bringing us to Christ.

In addition to these, the temple can also serve as a refuge during the storms of life. The temple helped me tremendously through some of the most difficult years of my life. I often found solace and refuge within its walls. Many of the most spiritual experiences of my life have occurred at the temple. The Savior Himself testified: "I will manifest myself to my people in mercy in this house" (see D&C 110:7). Come to the temple to seek His Spirit, His love, His mercy, and His solace in your life. Come to His house to find Him.

Chapter 7

YOUR ENDOWMENT

*O*ur modern western culture tends to be direct, straightforward, and largely void of symbolism and ritual. Particularly in the United States, we are a bottom-line oriented, get-to-the-point kind of people. Those traits sometimes spill over into our church experience as well. The temple endowment, on the other hand, reflects a very different culture and environment—one much closer to that found in heavenly realms. The temple is steeped in both symbolism and ritual. There, time and eternity meet. Past, present, and future are brought together as one. This transition can leave first-time attendees feeling a little disoriented and even culture-shocked. Add to this a lack of adequate preparation and not knowing what to expect, and some members leave the temple for the first time confused, disappointed, or even not wanting to return.

During my own endowment, I remember feeling the Spirit to a greater degree than ever before in my life. As a result, I left the temple knowing that it was a spiritually significant event. However, I didn't understand it and I found myself wondering: *what was that all about?* It took many years of temple attendance and a lot of study before it really started to make sense to me. For me, that understanding could have come much sooner with a little bit of help. It is my hope that this book gives you a head start in your own journey to understanding the temple.

Your First Time

Please don't let any of these ideas about your temple endowment discourage or overwhelm you. The best advice for someone going to the temple for the first time is to simply relax and enjoy the rich outpouring of the Spirit that you will experience. Don't worry about trying to remember everything because you won't. You will have a guide to help you at each step along the way. And you will be able to return over and over to do work for the dead, providing an opportunity for you to learn and understand the ceremony a little bit more each time. Accept the ordinances in faith. Over time, strive to understand them better and seek to implement them in your life. Initially, the most crucial parts are the covenants, and they are plain and easy to understand.

The ordinances of the temple are primarily associated with spiritual growth and maturation. Yet, even in the temple, the basic principles of the doctrine of Christ still undergird everything. Paul testified, "Therefore *not* leaving the principles of the doctrine of Christ, let us go on unto perfection" (JST Hebrews 6:1; emphasis added).[33] We never outgrow faith, repentance, baptism, and the Holy Ghost. The Holy Ghost is crucial to unlocking the temple's message in your life, and the doctrine of Christ becomes more important to our progression than ever. Don't imagine you get to set it aside. Rather, the ordinances of the temple will help you mature in it and in your discipleship on the path. In one sense, the temple ordinances are those of enduring to the end.

The Initiatory Ordinances

Your temple endowment actually begins with the initiatory ordinances. To help you understand them, consider a newborn infant for a moment. When a baby is physically born into the world, the baby is washed clean after the birth. The baby's skin may then be anointed with lotion or oil to protect it. He or she is then clothed and named. All of this is part of our entry into this mortal, physical world.

Baptism, of water and then of fire and the Holy Ghost, represents spiritual birth into God's kingdom. The next ordinances of the temple, referred to as the initiatory ordinances, continue this process of being born again and mirror your physical birth. First, you are washed clean. You are then anointed to become a king and a priest or a queen and a priestess unto

God. Next you are clothed in a holy garment and given a new name. All of this is part of your spiritual rebirth into God's kingdom.

The ordinance of baptism is a simple physical action with profound spiritual significance. The temple ordinances are likewise simple in their physical manifestations but carry rich spiritual meaning. President David O. McKay explained the initiatory ordinances: "After the preliminaries, you will be asked to go into a room where you will be washed. Now that act of washing in itself will be insignificant. There may be some things associated with it which you might criticize. But what is the significance of it? Cleanliness. . . . And then listen to why you are washed. The blessings that will come to your eyesight, to your mind, to your hearing."[34]

At baptism, some blessings are immediate, for example, a remission of sins and a greater access to the Holy Ghost. Other blessings are also promised but remain in the future. Baptism is the gate putting you on a path that eventually leads to eternal life, and this future blessing is dependent upon your continued faithfulness on the path. It is the same with the initiatory ordinances. In them you receive blessings that will strengthen and assist you in accomplishing your life's mission here and now, but they primarily prepare you for blessings in the resurrection.

President McKay continued his explanation of the initiatory: "The next little simple ceremony, I will call it little and simple because you might in your heart also consider it, is the Anointing. . . . But let your spiritual eyes see the significance of that anointing, and then you will realize what it means to be initiated into the House of God and all its mysteries." What is the purpose of this anointing? You are "anointed to become a king and a priest of the Most High; a queen and priestess in the realms of God. Now that is what it means. I do not know how long it will take you or me to achieve that, but we are anointed that we may become such."[35]

Once you have received these ordinances as a new *initiate* into God's kingdom, you are then prepared for the rest of your temple endowment which President McKay called the "truest philosophy of life ever given to man."[36] The endowment ceremony, when seen for what it is, "is the step-by-step ascent into the Eternal presence. If our young people could but glimpse it, it would be the most powerful spiritual motivation of their lives."[37] Following your spiritual birth into God's kingdom, the endowment is given to aid your spiritual growth, maturity, and upward climb back to God's presence.

Your Endowment: The Path Back to God

The endowment presentation is highly symbolic with layer upon layer of meaning and can be considered from multiple viewpoints. It offers more than we can grasp in a single session, which is one reason that it is a blessing to us to be able to return and do work for the deceased. Even after attending for many years, the temple can still offer us more if we remain teachable. Part of the genius and beauty of the symbolism in the temple is that it allows the Lord to personalize the experience to your individual needs and circumstances. As you grow and mature in your understanding over time, the endowment can still continue to teach and instruct. Please don't feel like you need to comprehend or remember it all on your first visit.

Since you are anointed to become a king or a queen in the initiatory ordinances, one way you can view the endowment is as a coronation ceremony.[38] Or, in other words, as an outlining of the steps Christ took in serving as the King and that you must follow to truly become a king or a queen. The anointing received in the initiatory is only *that you may eventually become* such. It is preparatory. It is a promise of a future event. It requires your subsequent faithfulness in following the path outlined in the endowment presentation.

In his book, *The House of the Lord*, Elder James E. Talmage briefly summarized the endowment as follows:

> This course of instruction includes a recital of the most prominent events of the creative period [the creation of the earth], the condition of our first parents in the Garden of Eden, their disobedience and consequent expulsion from that blissful abode, their condition in the lone and dreary world when doomed to live by labor and sweat, the plan of redemption by which the great transgression may be atoned, the period of the great apostasy, the restoration of the Gospel with all its ancient powers and privileges, the absolute and indispensable condition of personal purity and devotion to the right in present life, and a strict compliance with Gospel requirements.[39]

Viewing the endowment as an overview of history as Elder Talmage suggests is certainly helpful. For many years this was the only way I saw the endowment, but it is not the only way to interpret it.

In our modern temples, the endowment ceremony is generally presented through a film and audio presentation. You participate along with many others in an audience. It begins with the story of the Creation and the events in the Garden of Eden. In the days before film, actors played out the various roles in a drama before the company. That is still the case in the Salt Lake and Manti Utah Temples. In contrast, many who received their endowments in Nauvoo during the pioneer era actually participated in the ceremony by acting in the role of Adam or Eve. This provides us a clue to the meaning the endowment should hold for us. It is not meant simply as a history lesson. Rather, Adam and Eve are symbolic representations of our own individual lives. The endowment dialogue reinforces this idea by stating that throughout the presentation we must consider ourselves respectively as Adam and Eve.

This means that the endowment isn't just about "history"; it's primarily "your" story. You should relate it to your own life. God created you. Like Adam and Eve, you also began life in a state of innocence and belief, but as you grew and matured, you partook of sin and fell from that state. You must learn to return to God's presence and be redeemed just as our first parents were. The endowment is given to show us how.

The creation of the earth was first spiritual and then physical (see Moses 3:5). Likewise, when the Church builds a temple, a detailed blueprint is first created. Construction then proceeds according to the plan. Like the earth, a temple is first created spiritually (the blueprint) and then physically (the building). In like manner, your temple endowment is also a spiritual creation. You receive your blueprint in the temple. You then return to your daily life to perform the actual construction. The events you enact through ceremony in the endowment are meant for you to eventually experience in life as well. It was many years after being endowed before I recognized and understood that concept. If you miss it, you miss the whole point.

In chapter 9, we will cover the actual covenants and obligations that you will take upon yourself as part of your endowment experience. But before doing so, let's consider an important lesson we can learn from the temple ceremonies of ancient Israel, one which has a direct bearing on our own temple experience. Their temple ceremonies were largely intended to testify of and to point to Christ's future Atonement. Our rites also testify of Christ, but primarily show the way for us to return to Him. We are going to discuss just one of their ceremonies, The Day of Atonement. As we do so, watch for how beautifully the elements of the ceremony testify of and symbolize actual events of the Savior's life. See how the ceremony mirrored reality.

The Day of Atonement

Once a year, ancient Israel observed the Day of Atonement through a ceremony outlined in Leviticus chapter 16.[40] On this day, the high priest symbolically entered the presence of God and acted as a mediator for all of Israel. The scriptures explain that the purpose of this day was to cleanse the high priest, the tabernacle, the altar, all of the other priests, and the people in the congregation (see Leviticus 16:30, 33). In other words it was to purify and make holy the temple, the priesthood, and all of Israel through the high priest offering an atonement.

To understand the events of this day, you first need to know the basic layout of Moses's tabernacle, which served as a portable temple for the Israelites while wandering in the wilderness. The tabernacle was divided into three main areas—the outer court, the holy place, and the Holy of Holies—corresponding with the telestial, terrestrial, and celestial realms and representing increasing levels of holiness.[41]

1. The Outer Court: This was the largest of the three areas and the one where the sacrifices took place. The altar was located here along with vessels for washing. Priests and Israelites mingled here in performing the rites. This space represented the telestial realm.

2. The Holy Place: This was immediately inside the inner tent or the temple building. In it was a table containing sacred items including the shewbread (the bread of life), an altar of incense (the prayers of Israel), and the Menorah (a seven-branched candlestick representing the tree of life). Into this area the priests alone were permitted to enter. They did so twice daily, once in the morning and again in the evening to burn incense, light the candles, and replace the shewbread. This area represented the terrestrial realm.

3. The Holy of Holies or The Holy Place within the Veil: This area was the smallest part and its dimensions formed a perfect cube. It was the most holy or sacred spot in Judaism and represented the celestial realm. Here was kept the ark of the covenant with the original Ten Commandments. The ark represented not only the covenant between God and Israel but also the throne of God and His presence in Israel. Into this most sacred place only the high priest was permitted to enter, and then only once a year on the Day of Atonement.

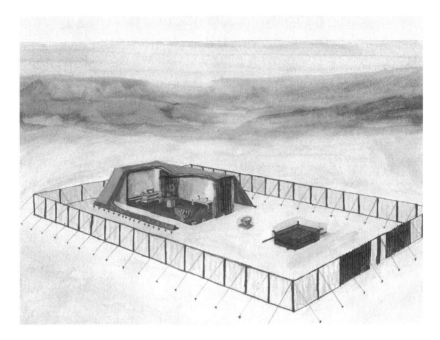

The tabernacle became the model for the later temple built by King Solomon. The tabernacle and Israel's subsequent temples functioned under the Aaronic Priesthood. The high priest in those days was the head of the Aaronic Priesthood.[42] Aaron served as the first high priest under Moses.

The Lord commanded Moses that on the tenth day of the seventh month there was to be a day of Atonement in Israel (see Leviticus 23:26–28). This was the only day the high priest could enter the Holy of Holies. The date was symbolic: ten pointed Israel to the Ten Commandments given at Sinai (which were the terms and conditions of the covenant between God and Israel), and seven represented the number of the days of creation, and as a number, seven signifies perfection, completion, and wholeness. So these two numbers together were intended to remind them of the significance of the day.

On the Day of Atonement, the high priest was to enter the Holy of Holies carrying a brazier of coals from the altar of sacrifice. Once inside, he placed incense on the coals, producing smoke. The rising smoke symbolized the prayers of Israel ascending to heaven. As the column of smoke reached the ceiling and began to fan out, it would briefly symbolize the tree of life found in the Garden of Eden. The area was so small, however, that smoke would quickly fill the room, forming a cloud. The Lord explained,

"And he shall put the incense upon the fire before the Lord, that the cloud of the incense may cover the mercy seat" (Leviticus 16:13).

In this action by the high priest we find elements from Sinai. The cloud of smoke represented the bright cloud associated with God's presence. Inside that cloud, the high priest symbolically stood in the presence of God, a clear symbolic recreation of Moses upon the mount. "And Moses went up into the mount, and a cloud covered the mount. And the glory of the Lord abode upon mount Sinai, and the cloud covered it *six* days: and the *seventh* day he called unto Moses out of the midst of the cloud. . . . And Moses went into the midst of the cloud" (Exodus 24:15–16, 18; emphasis added). Keep in mind this timing involving the sixth and the seventh days.

Burning the incense in the Holy of Holies reminded Israel of Moses's experience on Sinai. But it also foreshadowed the Messiah's future life as well. Matthew records,

> And after *six* days [i.e. on the *seventh*] Jesus taketh Peter, James, and John his brother, and bringeth them up into a high mountain apart,
>
> And was transfigured before them: and his face did shine as the sun, and his raiment was white as the light . . . [and] while he yet spake, behold, a *bright cloud overshadowed* them: and behold a voice out of the cloud, which said, This is my beloved Son, in whom I am well pleased; hear ye him.
>
> And when the disciples heard it, they fell on their face and were sore afraid. (Matthew 17:1–2, 5–6; emphasis added)

Christ entered into the Father's presence. What the high priest enacted symbolically, Christ experienced in reality. This action on the Day of Atonement was a testimony built into the Law of Moses that Christ would later fulfill.

Following the burning of the incense, the high priest was required to sacrifice two animals. One was a bullock (a bull) and the other a goat (a ram). First, he sacrificed the bullock. He was given three very specific instructions in connection with this sacrifice: 1) Bring some of the blood of this animal into the Holy of Holies and *sprinkle* it on the *east* part of the mercy seat; 2) Using his finger, he was then to sprinkle some of the blood on the *ground* before the mercy seat *seven times*; and 3) He was to be *alone* when he did this. There was to be no one else anywhere in the tabernacle until the high priest came back out. The rest of Israel waited completely outside (see Leviticus 16:14–17).

Now the questions naturally arise: why? Why such specific instructions regarding this particular sacrifice? What was it meant to teach? Once again, we find the answer in the final week of Christ's life. His suffering in the Garden of Gethsemane corresponds to this symbolic sacrifice of the bull. Luke records that Christ went to the Mount of Olives, which was located *east* of the temple. Similarly, the high priest sprinkled blood on the *east* side of the mercy seat. Luke then tells us that Christ "being in an agony he prayed more earnestly: and his sweat was as it were great drops of blood falling down to the ground" (Luke 22:44). During His Atonement, Christ suffered and bled, *sprinkling* His blood upon the ground in a perfect sacrifice just as the high priest *sprinkled* the blood of the bull on the ground in front of the mercy seat. Lastly, Christ was alone during these events. No man accompanied Him. His waiting disciples were about a stone's throw away and asleep (see Luke 22:41). In a symbolic recreation of this moment, when the high priest likewise sprinkled the blood of the bull on the ground in front of the mercy seat, all of Israel waited outside the tabernacle of the congregation—about a stone's throw away. There is a perfect correlation between Christ's atoning sacrifice and the symbols of the Day of Atonement.

Following the sacrifice of the bullock, the high priest was to then take two goats and present them before the congregation at the door of the tabernacle. He cast lots upon the two goats, one for the Lord and the other for a scapegoat. The goat upon which the Lord's lot fell, he offered up as a sacrifice. But the other, the scapegoat, was laden with Israel's sins and set free (see Leviticus 16:7–10, 20–22).

Returning, once again, to the account in Luke, we find this event again reflects the Savior's last days. Christ and Barabbas were both presented before the congregation. Two men are presented before Israel, just as the two goats had been. Luke records,

> They cried out all at once saying, Away with this man, and release unto us Barabbas:
> (Who for a certain sedition made in the city, and for murder, was cast into prison.)
> Pilate therefore, willing to release Jesus, spake again unto them.
> But they cried, saying, Crucify him, crucify him.
> And he said unto them the third time, Why, what evil hath he done? I have found no cause of death in him: I will therefore chastise him, and let him go.

And they were instant with loud voices, requiring that he might be crucified. And the voices of them and of the chief priests prevailed.

And [Pilate] released unto them him that for sedition and murder was cast into prison, whom they had desired; but he delivered Jesus to their will. (Luke 23:18–23, 25)

One was sacrificed and the other released, the choice being made before the congregation. One was literally the Son of the Father. The other's name, ironically, is comprised of two words: "Bar" meaning "the son of" and "Abba" meaning "father." So in these two men presented before Israel we find the actual Son of God on one hand and another who is also a son of God. Barabbas stood as a symbol for each of us as God's children: guilty. Christ stood innocent.

Once the choice had been made, Christ was sacrificed for sin, while Barabbas laden with sins was set free. On the Day of Atonement, the goat, representing the Savior, was sacrificed by the high priest, and his blood was carried into the Holy of Holies and sprinkled in a manner similar to the bull's blood.

In the sacrifice of these two animals, the bullock and the ram, we see symbols of the two parts of the Savior's Atonement, first as He suffered in the Garden and then again as He suffered on the cross. After both sacrifices, the high priest carried the blood of the sacrifice into the Holy of Holies and sprinkled it before the Father to be accepted. When the actual Atonement occurred, as Christ completed His sacrifice, the Father Himself opened the Holy of Holies to acknowledge and to accept His son's perfect offering. Matthew simply states, "And, behold, the veil of the temple was rent in twain from the top to the bottom; and the earth did quake, and the rocks rent" (Matthew 27:51).

In every detail, Christ conformed perfectly to the Father's great plan. His final week fulfills every element of the symbolism He built into the Day of Atonement rites revealed to Moses. Do you see how the ceremony reflected and taught the later reality?

OUR TEMPLE RITES

If you are not yet endowed, please be assured that although the ancient Israelites practiced animal sacrifices and had literal washings and anointings, our temple ordinances are more symbolic in nature. There is no shedding or use of blood in our temples. Modesty is likewise preserved throughout the experience. Despite anything you may have read or heard to the contrary, nothing in your temple experience should leave you uncomfortable. You will also have a guide to help you throughout the process. With that said, let's return to the lesson we need to learn from the Day of Atonement for our own temple experience.

The law of Moses with its ceremonies, rites, and ordinances was meant to be a schoolmaster to bring Israel unto Christ (see Galatians 3:24). Without Christ, the law of Moses was powerless. Unfortunately, many of the ancient Israelites failed to grasp what the law of Moses was designed to teach. Many participated in the Day of Atonement believing it was the animal sacrifices of the bull and the goat that actually cleansed Israel. In doing so, they completely missed the point. King Benjamin testified to his people that "holy prophets spake unto them concerning his coming; and yet they hardened their hearts, and understood not that the law of Moses availeth nothing except it were through the atonement of his blood" (Mosiah 3:15). Without Christ's real Atonement, the sacrifices Israel offered were meaningless.

Each element of our own temple ceremony, in like manner, also points to greater realities. With that in mind, we might well ask: what is the purpose of our own temple endowment? And how do we avoid participating in it but missing the intent as did many of the ancient Israelites? Those are questions that you will need to grapple with and answer for yourself. To help you get started in thinking about these things, I will simply repeat that, in my view, there are three primary purposes for our temple endowment: One is to testify of Christ. The second is to complete our spiritual rebirth and help us grow into spiritual maturity. And the third purpose is to bring us unto Christ to be redeemed by Him. As you have the opportunity to attend the temple, ponder on what the ordinances mean to you and how they can unfold in your own life.

ADAM AND EVE'S EXPERIENCE

If this sounds like some work ahead of you, it is. It is not enough to simply go through the temple once and then set it aside. We tend to value what we work and struggle for, and we all need the joy of discovery. I believe the Lord intends for these things to unfold line upon line to us as we seek for greater understanding. The whole process is richly rewarding, and the blessings obtained are worth the price. This book is simply meant to help give you a foundation from which to begin.

Perhaps Adam and Eve's experience is instructive for each of us as well. When Adam and Eve were cast out of Eden, the Lord commanded them to offer sacrifices. They did this in faith for years without understanding why. After many days, an angel explained the meaning and purpose behind the sacrifices, and they at last understood (see Moses 5:6). It may be the same for us. Go to the temple and accept the ordinances in faith even though you won't understand everything at first. Trust that there is meaning behind what you are doing and that in time you can come to understand it. Return to the temple often and ask the Lord to teach you more. I testify that He will. Be patient with the process. We may participate for many years without fully understanding it, but eventually the Lord helps us to see more. For me, much of that has come line upon line, a little at a time. In the meanwhile, regular, purposeful temple attendance will bless your life, transform your character, and provide strength through life's storms.

BARRIERS TO LEARNING

The Lord intends the temple to be a house of learning, and we are commanded to seek learning by study and also by faith (see D&C 109:7–8). I believe with all of my heart that the Lord wants us to come to fully understand the endowment here in this life. We receive it here and it should be understood here, even though that requires some effort and work on our part.

Three things may hinder our learning. One barrier is simply a lack of interest. We can become too busy with other things in life to give the temple much of our time and attention. This can deprive us of choice knowledge the Lord is willing to bestow.

Another barrier to learning is thinking we already know enough—we then stop inquiring and seeking for more. Rather, we must remain as little children and continually be open to being taught. No matter how much we have already gained, the Lord is willing to offer us more and the temple has more to offer. Some people say that they learn something new every time they attend the temple. It has not been that way for me, but insights have come with persistent effort and attendance. Elder John A. Widtsoe taught:

> Revelation . . . is not imposed upon a person; it must be drawn to us by faith, seeking and working. . . . To the man or woman who goes through the temple, with open eyes, heeding the symbols and the covenants, and making a steady, continuous effort to understand the full meaning, God speaks his word, and revelations come. . . . The

endowment which was given by revelation can best be understood by revelation; and to those who seek most vigorously, with pure hearts, will the revelation be greatest.[43]

Finally, the learning we can receive from the temple is dramatically hindered by the idea that we aren't meant to understand the endowment in this life but it will finally make sense in the next life. The notion that we will finally "get it" in the next life is a mistake, though it may be a commonly held belief and one that I shared for many years. It seems reinforced by Brigham Young's statement about the endowment. He said, "Your endowment is, to receive all those ordinances in the house of the Lord, which are necessary for you . . . to enable you to walk back to the presence of the Father, passing the angels who stand as sentinels, being enabled to give them the key words, the signs and the tokens, pertaining to the holy Priesthood, and gain your eternal exaltation."[44] On the surface, this statement appears to mean that you need to learn and memorize the signs and tokens given in the temple, and then you will be able to use them in the next life. Many members attend long enough to memorize these things and then feel that they have obtained enough.

I used to believe that the challenge of this life was becoming worthy of and then staying worthy of a temple recommend. Once in the temple, you then received information (key words, tokens, and signs) that would act as a kind of *recommend* in the next life. You would use them to pass by the angel sentinels. That idea may be widely shared among the Saints. You are completely free to believe that, as I once did, but today I don't view it that way at all. Let me explain why. Please pardon me if this next statement seems offensive to you, but I don't know a better way to put it. Your endowment is not about receiving some *magic passwords* any more than temple garments are *magic underwear*, as is sometimes portrayed.

Think about it for a moment. If we take Brigham's statement literally, then any man or woman can go to the temple and receive their endowment (or worse, just look it up online). They could carefully memorize and keep in their memory what they were taught, but could then come out of the temple, break all of their covenants, and live a wicked life. After death, as long as they remembered the temple's tokens and signs, they could pass by the angels and gain their exaltation in the next life despite having made no effort to keep their covenants. Such a notion is completely nonsensical. So the endowment must not mean that. There must be something else.

Once we recognize that the tokens and signs of the priesthood given in the temple are symbols, then you can see that what is really important is coming to understand what the symbols represent and then receiving those actual things in your life. If you receive, not just the symbol, but also that which it represents, then you will be able to pass by the angels. So Brigham's statement is technically correct, but perhaps widely misunderstood.[45] Similarly, Elder Widtsoe testified, "No man or woman can come out of the temple endowed as he should be, unless he has seen, beyond the symbol, the mighty realities for which the symbols stand."[46] We must not only come to see but also actually receive these realities in our lives. If we fail to do so, we are no better off than the ancient Israelites who participated in their ceremonies without any real comprehension of their true meaning.

When you go to the temple and come back into the world, work on living and implementing your covenants in your day-to-day life. Consecrate yourself to the Lord. Over time you will come to understand and, more important, to actually receive the blessings that the tokens represent. If you do that, then you will be able to pass by the angels and gain your exaltation. Ask the Lord to teach you. Have faith that He will.

HOMEWORK

1. Ponder on why you want to be endowed. Discuss that with your parents, friends, and Church leaders. It shouldn't just be something that you automatically do before a mission or a marriage. It should be a special and important event in its own right. What could you do to make it that way?

2. If you are preparing to go to the temple for your own endowment, I would recommend you read chapter 3 of *Understanding Your Endowment* before you go. It contains a much more detailed discussion of the how and why of the initiatory ordinances. It will help you know what to expect and what it means.

3. For a more complete discussion of the endowment's meaning, read chapter 4 of *Understanding Your Endowment*. You may want to wait to read it until after you have attended a few times.

4. Consider these promises given us for temple service. For many years, I have treasured these promises and can testify that they have been fulfilled in my life:

+ The Prophet Joseph Smith: "Being born again, comes by
  the Spirit of God through ordinances."[47]
+ President Gordon B. Hinckley: "I urge our people everywhere, with all of the persuasiveness of which I am capable,
  to live worthy to hold a temple recommend, to secure one
  and regard it as a precious asset, and to make a greater effort
  to go to the house of the Lord and partake of the spirit and
  blessings to be had therein. I am satisfied that every man or
  woman who goes to the temple in a spirit of sincerity and
  faith leaves the house of the Lord a better man or woman.
  There is need for constant improvement in all of our lives.
  There is need occasionally to leave the noise and the tumult
  of the world and step within the walls of a sacred house of
  God, there to feel His spirit in an environment of holiness
  and peace."[48]
+ Sister Silvia H. Allred, former first counselor in the Relief
  Society General Presidency: "The temple is a house of
  learning. Much of the instruction imparted in the temple
  is symbolic and learned by the Spirit. This means we are
  taught from on high. Temple covenants and ordinances are
  a powerful symbol of Christ and His Atonement. We all
  receive the same instruction, but our understanding of the
  meaning of the ordinances and covenants will increase as
  we return to the temple often with the attitude of learning
  and contemplating the eternal truths taught."[49]
+ Elder Boyd K. Packer: "Our labors in the temple cover us
  with a shield and a protection, both individually and as a
  people. . . . The Lord will bless us as we attend to the sacred
  ordinance work of the temples. Blessings there will not be
  limited to our temple service. We will be blessed in all of
  our affairs. We will be eligible to have the Lord take an
  interest in our affairs both spiritual and temporal."[50]
+ President Gordon B. Hinckley: "I would hope that we
  might go to the house of the Lord a little more frequently.
  . . . I encourage you to take greater advantage of this blessed
  privilege. It will refine your natures. It will peel off the self-
  ish shell in which most of us live. It will literally bring a

sanctifying element into our lives and make us better men and women."[51]

+ Sister Ardeth G. Kapp, former Young Women General President: "In the temple you will gain a clearer understanding and appreciation of who you really are. It is there that you will learn more about the Savior than anywhere else I know."[52]

+ President Ezra Taft Benson: "Many parents, in and out of the Church, are concerned about protection against a cascading avalanche of wickedness which threatens to engulf [the world]. . . . There is a power associated with ordinances of heaven—even the power of godliness—which can and will thwart the forces of evil if we will but be worthy of those sacred [covenants made in the temple of the Lord.]"[53]

+ Elder John A. Widtsoe speaking of the blessings that come from temple worship: "At the most unexpected moments, in or out of the temple will come to him [or her], as a revelation, the solution of the problems that vex his [or her] life."[54]

+ Sister Ardeth G. Kapp: "In the temple, the reality of eternity presses upon our minds. When we learn to view our experiences in this life with the perspective of eternity, we tend to draw away from the things of the world that pull us apart, and to feel closer to the things of the Spirit that keep us whole. We begin to view life differently."[55]

Chapter 8
SYMBOLISM

The Lord built symbolism into the ordinances of the gospel. This is especially true of the temple ordinances. Because the endowment is highly symbolic, we will discuss some of the symbols you need to understand in this chapter. Knowing them will give you a basic "temple vocabulary." Because symbolism is such an important topic to the temple, I addressed it briefly in *Understanding Your Endowment*. Please forgive the repetition of some of that material here. It is important background for the more expanded discussion of symbolism, which follows in this volume.

WHY SYMBOLS?

Consider for a moment the difference between a routine and a ritual. Both can be something that we participate in often. Both may be repetitive. For example, you might have a daily routine in the morning as you rise from bed and prepare for your day. You probably go through it automatically without much thought.

A ritual, on the other hand, can hold deep meaning in our lives. We participate in rituals purposefully and with understanding of the underlying intent the ritual portrays. If we aren't careful, we can find ourselves participating in gospel ordinances, such as the sacrament, as a routine rather than a ritual. As we come to appreciate the symbolism built into gospel ordinances and the underlying realities associated with those symbols, then participating in gospel ordinances can move from a thoughtless routine to a sacred ritual we cherish.

During the Savior's lifetime He often taught with parables. These stories were easy to remember and on the surface appeared fairly simple. The underlying truths they contained were profound. Parables sometimes condense complex concepts into their core essence. Gospel ordinances are the same. It should not be a surprise then that the Lord's house is filled with symbolism. Still, we might wonder why the Lord uses symbols in His teachings. Here are a few reasons. Perhaps you can think of others as well.

1. Symbols encourage us to have a prayerful, searching attitude.
2. Symbols can leave a longer, more powerful impression upon our minds than words alone.
3. A great deal of information can be encoded into a simple symbol. Most symbols are multifaceted and have multiple meanings. Many symbols contain both negative and positive connotations and can provide both a warning and a promised blessing in one symbol. When it comes to the gospel, it is easy to underestimate how much a single symbol can contain. Don't worry if your understanding of a symbol is different from another person's understanding of it. Both of you may be correct.
4. Symbols protect the sacred and prevent us from being accountable for truths we are not yet prepared to receive (see Matthew 13:10–13).
5. Symbols are more universal and timeless than language and can more easily bridge differences in culture, language, nationality, age, and so on.
6. Symbols capture commonalities of the human condition, while still allowing for our individual experience, interpretation, and adaptation. By using symbols, the Lord is able to make the temple both universal and at the same time very personal to each of His children.
7. Perhaps one of the greatest reasons for symbols in the temple is to allow the Lord to customize and personalize your endowment to you. As you grow and your understanding increases over time, He can reveal more to you.

For these reasons, symbols can sometimes communicate more effectively than words. Symbols can also be adapted or changed by their context. Take the symbol of a heart as an example.

This little drawing can represent a physical organ in our body, but more often it is associated with complex feelings such as love or courage. It can also be associated with the spiritual or moral core of a person.

By adding a jagged line to this symbol, we completely change the meaning. Now we have a broken heart. Most of us have experienced a broken heart and so this little drawing on a page might bring to our minds painful past memories and emotions.

Add an arrow to the original heart, and the meaning is changed again, this time to represent romantic love.

In all of this, the important thing is to not confuse or mistake the symbol with the thing being symbolized. If we only see the *hearts* and miss the realities of courage, love, romance, or heartache that are represented, then we have missed the purpose of the symbol.

The same principle applies when you attend the temple. It may take some time for you to connect the symbols with their underlying truths, but don't be content simply to learn the symbols. Recognize that you also need to eventually see what they are trying to teach.

May I suggest a few principles, which you may find helpful: First, recognize that many symbols teach us of the Savior. "And behold, all things have their likeness, and all things are created and made to bear record of me, both things which are temporal and things which are spiritual" (Moses 6:63). This is especially true in His house. As you encounter symbols in the temple, ask yourself what they teach you about Christ and your relationship with Him. As we discussed earlier, the temple contains one of the greatest testimonies of the Savior in all of the Restoration. However, it took me many years and required some help for me to see it. Don't be discouraged if it is not immediately apparent to you. The most critical parts of your endowment, the covenants, are plain and easy to grasp. Focus on them first.

Second, symbols present an opportunity to learn. Whenever you encounter symbolism, whether it is found in the scriptures or in the temple, there exists an invitation to receive more knowledge through revelation. The Lord took the trouble to encode these things, and the Spirit can help you decode them. Ask the Lord to teach you. And be patient. The answers will generally come line upon line.

Third, don't limit the Lord's use of symbols. One mistake I made for many years was thinking in terms of X symbol must equal Y symbol (X=Y). I was looking for a single meaning for each symbol and failed to recognize the fact that most symbols have layer upon layer of meaning. It would be more accurate to say X equals Y and Z and A and B and D and Q and S.

Symbols may have both negative and positive meanings. For example, in the previous discussion on the Day of Atonement, the high priest performed the ceremonies. In that role, he symbolized Christ who is the great High Priest (see Hebrews 3:1). Christ ultimately would make an intercession for all of Israel. In their roles, Aaron and the other high priests were simply types pointing to Him. But notice at the same time, they were also the ones who actually killed the sacrificial animal. And as such, they also foreshadowed Annas and Caiaphas and the wicked, apostate priesthood that would eventually condemn our Lord and send Him to His death. In the person of the high priest on the Day of Atonement, we find both a symbol of Christ and those who would kill Him.

Another great example of how vast the Lord's use of symbolism can be is found in the vision of Lehi.[56] The vision makes up one chapter in the Book of Mormon and is filled with simple day-to-day symbols (see 1 Nephi 8). Lehi interpreted and explained these symbols primarily as they related to his own family. We often do likewise in our Sunday School lessons and apply them to our own spiritual journey through life. Lehi didn't explain everything, however. Nephi still had questions about the vision so he asked for and was given an explanation of the symbols. Nephi testified that he saw exactly the same things his father saw (see 1 Nephi 11:3, 14:29), and yet Nephi's vision covers four chapters (see 1 Nephi 11–14). The explanation of these same symbols to Nephi included the Savior's birth, life and ministry, the twelve Apostles, the land of promise and its inhabitants, the Savior's visit to the Americas, and much of the history of the world including the founding of America, the Restoration of the gospel, and the winding-up scenes before the Second Coming. All of this information was also contained in the symbols of Lehi's dream. In the temple endowment presentation, we are given the simplified Lehi dream version, but the expanded Nephi version is there as well. In order to see it, we must ask the Lord for help as did Nephi.

Finally, and perhaps most important, apply the symbols to yourself. As Nephi did with the scriptures, liken the symbols of the temple to your life. One of the most imperative reasons the Lord uses symbols is that they can be very personal and individual. Despite our many similarities, we are all unique. We bring different backgrounds, experiences, needs, and levels of understanding with us to the temple. By using symbols, the Lord can personalize the endowment for each of us. Your understanding of a particular symbol may be different from mine and both may be correct.

COMMON GOSPEL SYMBOLS

You should gain at least a basic understanding of some common symbols found throughout the scriptures and in the temple. Like the parables that Christ taught, many symbols are ordinary everyday things but with special meaning in the gospel. Even common things like numbers and colors have symbolic significance.

Understanding symbols will help bring greater meaning to your temple worship and to the ordinances of the gospel. Pondering on their meaning can help you gain deeper insights into the purpose of the ordinance. The sacrament is a good example. The symbols are simple but as we partake, their implications are profound.

Below is a brief discussion of a few symbols that you may find helpful as you go to the temple. As we proceed, again, please keep two cautions in mind: First, nearly all symbols have multiple meanings. Please don't limit the Lord's use of them in teaching you. Just because you already understand one or more sets of meanings with a symbol doesn't mean that there aren't more. The summaries, which follow, are simply a good starting point. They are not comprehensive. A second caution is to keep these things in perspective. While they can be very helpful in adding richness and depth to our worship, we shouldn't get so focused on them that they become a giant game of gospel trivia. Nor should we get too frustrated by the things we don't yet understand. The important part is not understanding every little nuance of every little symbol, but actually living the endowment in our lives. The most crucial parts are plain to all. Begin with your focus there and let the other things come along in time.

With those two cautions, let's look at a few basic temple and scriptural symbols and their meanings:

COLORS: Many colors have symbolic meaning. For example, the color white symbolizes purity, holiness, cleanliness, righteousness, light, glory, and unity. Green is a symbol of life. Purple a symbol of royalty or nobility. Blue suggests the heavens. Scarlet or red is a symbol of the blood of sacrifice.

OLIVE OIL: Olive oil is a symbol of the Holy Ghost and its influence (see D&C 45:56–57). Olive trees were found in the Garden of Gethsemane, and the symbolism is therefore also tied to the Atonement and is also associated with revelation, healing, and consecration. The oil represents holy anointing by the power of the Spirit of God. The Apostle John wrote of God's Spirit as an "anointing." He declared, "But the anointing which ye have received of him abideth in you, and ye need not that any man teach you: but as the same anointing teacheth you of all things, and is truth, and is no lie, and even as it hath taught you, ye shall abide in him" (1 John 2:27).

HORN OF SALVATION: Horns are symbols of strength, honor, and power. Animals possessing horns rely upon them as their primary means of defense and attack. Under the law of Moses, the horns of the altar of burnt offerings were to be smeared with the blood of the sacrifice (see Exodus 29:12). Anciently, kings were anointed with oil from a horn (1 Samuel 16:1, 13). Christ is referred to as a "horn of salvation" (Luke 1:69) meaning that He is mighty to save.

ROBES: Anciently, robes indicated status and were tied to a person's identity.[57] For example, in the story of the prodigal son we see this concept illustrated when the wayward son returns expecting to be a servant, but instead finding his position in the household restored by the simple act of his father bringing forth a robe and clothing him (see Luke 15:22).

SHOES/SANDALS: Shoes were also part of a person's identity and together with the feet symbolized the course of one's life. The prodigal son received not only a robe, but also shoes from his father. John the Baptist indicated he was not worthy to unloose Christ's shoes. Moses was told to remove his shoes because he was entering holy ground. He was about to receive a new calling and direction for his life, walking on a new path and leaving his old life behind. Paul also taught that our feet should be shod with the gospel of peace as part of our spiritual armor (see Ephesians 6:15).

SERPENT: The serpent is another symbol with both positive and negative connotations. Originally, it was a symbol of Christ (see Helaman 8:14–15). Satan usurped this symbol in Eden in an attempt to play God and deceive Adam and Eve, and since then it has often been associated with him instead. Perhaps it seems odd that a serpent can symbolize Christ, but it is apt since a serpent's fangs can bring death, but a serpent can also shed its skin in a symbolic resurrection to new life. Thus a serpent is a symbol of both life and death. Christ is the God of both life and death. He established the conditions for mortality and our eventual death, but He also brought about the Resurrection and our immortality. Moses used a brazen serpent as a symbol of Christ while in the wilderness with the Israelites (see Numbers 21:8–9; Helaman 8:14–15).

PEOPLE: People can also serve as symbols or types, generally to foreshadow our Savior. For example, in the life of Jonah we see shadows of the Savior's life. Jonah was cast into the sea to die in order to save others. He was swallowed up and spent three days in the "belly of hell" before being brought forth (see Jonah 2:2). In Jonah's life, we see modeled sacrifice, the Fall, death, redemption, and the Resurrection. Eve also foreshadowed Christ. Her question "Is there no other way?" raised in the Garden of Eden was echoed millennia later by our Savior in another garden when facing the Atonement. There, He asked essentially the same question (see Matthew 26:39).

MOTHERS: Mothers (inclusive of all women) are also types of Christ. They reflect Him in at least three important ways: 1) Like Christ, mothers also shed their blood and descend into the vale of death to bring forth new life. 2) Paul taught that the veil of the temple is a symbol of Christ's flesh (see Hebrews 10:19–20). Given that, if Christ is the veil through which we must pass to eternal life, then I would submit that a mother's womb is the veil through which all mankind passes to enter mortal life. Mothers are a veil on one end of our journey while Christ is the veil on the other end. The temple endowment provides us with an important reminder of this truth as the sisters are veiled as part of their temple clothing. 3) A mother's love is often the closest thing a child experiences to God's own love for us and it is through a mother's love that we may first experience and begin to understand God's love. In these three ways, mothers are important types of Christ.

NUMBERS: (3, 7, 8, 9, 12, 40, etc.) Many numbers have symbolic meaning. For example, the number three can connote a beginning, middle, and an end; or past, present, and future. It also represents the degrees of our separation from God as a result of the Fall (telestial, terrestrial, and celestial). Three can symbolize the Godhead, or a presidency, or the law of witnesses. Seven is a symbol of completion or perfection. It is a complete cycle. Seven combines the number three of the heavens and the spirit with the number four of the earth and the body. There were seven periods in the Creation. There are seven days in the week. We find this number occurring in nature as well. For example, there are seven notes in a scale and seven colors in a rainbow. Because seven represents a full or complete cycle, eight marks the beginning of a new cycle. Eight is therefore associated with rebirth, resurrection, and renewal. Circumcision was done on the eighth day (see Leviticus 12:3). Baptism and accountability occur in the eighth year of life (see D&C 68:27). Christ was resurrected on the eighth day, and so on. Mathematically, nine symbolizes both everything and nothing, the finite and the infinite. In terms of physics, nine can represent both the gravitational singularity and the event horizon (or the beginning of the universe and its outer boundary).[58] It is not surprising then that we find this number tied to important things in life and the gospel. For example, a full-term human pregnancy requires nine months. Christ's sacrifice inflicted nine wounds (two on His hands, two on His wrists, two on His feet, one on His side, one on His back, and one on the crown of His head) and He died in the ninth hour of the day (see Luke 23:44). The number twelve is symbolic of priesthood. Multiples of twelve amplify this number so that twelve squared, or 144, is often associated with a fulness of the priesthood. Forty is a symbol for a period of purification or consecration. Israel wandered in the wilderness for forty years. Moses was upon the mount for forty days. The rains descended upon the ark for forty days and forty nights. And Christ spent forty days in the wilderness following His baptism.

There are many, many more and I would refer you to the homework section of this chapter for a good beginning reference on gospel symbolism.

THE TEMPLE THRESHOLD— AN EXAMPLE OF TEMPLE SYMBOLISM

LDS scholar Hugh Nibley once observed that the temple is a scale model of the universe.[59] At least in part, he seemed to have had the physical structure in mind. In other words, the buildings have something to testify of and to teach about. Many of our modern temples have three levels (basement, ground level, and upper floors). The Mount Timpanogos Utah Temple is a good example. In a general way, we could correlate these three levels to the underworld (or spirit world), the earth, and the heavens. In the Salt Lake Temple we find seven spiritual divisions or realms. These are represented by seven distinct areas or rooms in the Salt Lake Temple:

1. The temple threshold
2. The baptistry and initiatory ordinance room
3. The creation room
4. The garden room
5. The world or telestial room
6. The terrestrial room
7. The celestial room (including the sealing rooms)

These same seven divisions are present in other temples as well, although they are sometimes portrayed through changes in the endowment presentation (i.e. lighting, narration, and so on) rather than architecturally through separate and distinct rooms.[60]

The question is what are we to learn from the temple's architecture and layout? Let's look at just the first of these divisions—the temple threshold—and consider the symbolism associated with it. A threshold is something we often overlook and pay little attention to in our modern world, but anciently it was highly symbolic and very important.[61]

A threshold forms a boundary. Together with the posts, lintel, and door, it separates what lies outside from what lies inside. In ancient times, a home's threshold was sacred. One who crossed over the threshold was entitled, during his or her stay, to the hospitality and protection of those who were within the house. In the case of a very special guest, or when welcoming a new bride or groom to the family, a sacrifice was offered at the threshold. While the guest was still outside, the host would lay a sheep or goat upon the threshold of the house and offer it there as a sacrifice. The honored guest would then step over the blood and by this act become adopted as a recognized member of the family in what was known as a threshold covenant.[62] A remnant of this ancient welcome may still remain in our day when a groom traditionally lifts and carries his bride across the threshold into their new home. Once a threshold covenant was formed, the doorposts and lintel were sometimes marked with the blood from the sacrifice as proof of the covenant.[63]

Understanding this ancient tradition sheds new light on the Passover night of the Hebrew exodus from Egypt. "In dealing with his chosen people, God did not invent a new rite . . . but he took a rite with which they were already familiar, and gave to it a new and deeper significance."[64] For the Hebrew Passover, the chosen sacrifice was to be a lamb. Its blood was smeared on the doorposts and lintel as a welcome to Jehovah (see

Exodus 12:22) and as a declaration that Jehovah was the God of that household. The promise was that "when he seeth the blood upon the lintel, and on the two side posts, the Lord will pass over [cross over or through] the door, and will not suffer the destroyer to come in unto your houses to smite you" (Exodus 12:23). The Passover wasn't a sign to have Jehovah pass by the home; rather, it was a welcome for Him to enter as part of the family and to protect it. In this manner, Jehovah did not merely spare His people the judgment He visited on the Egyptians, but He renewed His covenant with them.[65]

Additionally, one could make an appeal for justice or hospitality by appearing at the gate or threshold of a home. Even an enemy could appeal for protection or for reconciliation in this manner.[66] It was likely no accident that Christ placed the beggar Lazarus at the rich man's gate in His parable rather than having the rich man encounter the beggar in the marketplace or at some other location (see Luke 16:19–31). The rich man's obligation to care for, and his condemnation for neglecting, were both made greater by Lazarus's appearance at the gate, which should have compelled the rich man to act, bringing Lazarus inside the gate threshold and ministering to his suffering. Following their deaths, the rich man finds the roles reversed, and he is now the one on the outside of a threshold or barrier, pleading for relief. Abraham informs him that the threshold found on the other side was a great gulf and that Lazarus cannot pass over (see Luke 16:26).

So how might these ancient ideas relate to our modern temples? While we may have lost sight of the significance of the threshold in our day, the Lord has not. In the dedicatory prayer of the Kirtland Temple, which was given by revelation, He stated, "And that all people who shall enter upon *the threshold of the Lord's house* may feel thy power, and feel constrained to acknowledge that thou has sanctified it, and that it is . . . a place of thy holiness" (D&C 109:13; emphasis added). The temple is set apart from the outside world, an intersecting place where time and eternity meet. Its threshold separates the spiritual within from the physical world without. We, like Lazarus, come to the temple's threshold as beggars appealing for reconciliation, protection, and relief. Unlike the rich man, the Lord does not turn us away from His house but welcomes us openly. Within temple walls, He freely ministers to our needs.

Ultimately, it is Christ Himself who is the door. He testified, "I am the door: by me if any man enter in, he shall be saved, and shall go in and out, and find pasture" (John 10:9). Recognize then as you approach the temple door that it is one of the first symbols of Christ you encounter in the temple. Consider what it means to pass over the temple threshold and enter within its walls as a guest. Can you approach reverently and sense the Lord's power and influence and holiness there?

The doors of the Mount Timpanogos Temple are covered with eight panels, as shown below.

As previously mentioned, eight is a number frequently associated with Christ. It symbolizes rebirth, renewal, starting over, the beginning of a new cycle, and resurrection. It is also associated with mediation between earth and heaven. It is no coincidence that there are eight panels on this temple door. Each panel contains a large flower, which I have been told represents a lotus blossom. Assuming that is true, the lotus flower is another potent symbol of Christ. This flower begins life submerged in a pond and emerges slowly over a three-day period from this watery grave to bloom in the morning sun of the third day. This flower is also associated with purity, spiritual awakening, and faithfulness.[67]

Furthermore, each flower on the temple door is comprised of eighteen petals. If you do the math, 8 flowers x 18 petals = 144 total petals. The number twelve is associated with priesthood, and by squaring the number, the meaning is amplified, so the number 144 suggests a fulness of the priesthood, which we also find in Christ.[68] So once again, the flowers and petals point our minds to Christ.

Finally, the brass or copper color of the door is symbolic of judgment.[69] This is also appropriate as a symbol of Christ since the "Father judgeth no man, but hath committed all judgment unto the Son" (John 5:22). And, "the keeper of the gate is the Holy One of Israel; and he employeth no servant there; and there is none other way save it be by the gate; for he cannot be deceived, for the Lord God is his name" (2 Nephi 9:41).

So just in the door of the Mount Timpanogos Utah Temple, we encounter symbols that testify of and can point our minds to Christ. We approach the temple threshold reverently, recognizing the great gulf between us and our Lord. In passing over, we leave the outside world behind and enter as His guests.

I close by repeating a word of caution. These kinds of symbols are found throughout the temple. They are interesting and can add depth and richness to our experience, but don't let them distract or frustrate you. The most important parts of the temple are plain and precious and easy to grasp. It is far more important to come to understand and live the covenants we make than it is to know the symbolism of the temple threshold and door. That being said, make an effort to understand the temple's ordinances and its symbolism over time.

Homework

1. Take the time and effort to learn basic gospel symbols. A good place to start is the website www.ldssymbols.com. Spend some time familiarizing yourself with the symbols found there. It contains a summary of common shapes, numbers, and colors. You will see many of them used in the Church's temples. You will also find many of them referred to in the scriptures.

Chapter 9
THE TEMPLE COVENANTS

In the endowment ceremony we make certain covenants with the Lord. Covenants are much more than two-way promises as is commonly understood. They create sacred, binding relationships. Anciently, covenants were formed through a ceremony in a series of specific steps that held meaning for the participants. Some of these ancient practices are found in our modern temple ceremony. For a more complete exploration of covenants and covenant ceremonies, please see chapter 1 of *Understanding Your Endowment*. This is an important topic to understand, but for our purposes here we will focus simply on the promise part of covenants.

During your endowment you made or will make five primary covenant promises to the Lord. (We also covenant not to disclose certain information that we receive in the temple. Those promises are in addition and are not counted as part of the five discussed here.) Sometimes, before entering the temple for the first time, members want to know what they will be committing to in the temple. What obligations am I taking upon myself as a result of going to the temple? Does the Lord expect something more of me after I am endowed? These seem to be reasonable concerns. Although the Church's temple preparation manual states that the instructor may list the endowment covenants on the chalkboard,[70] often that does not occur in the class. As a result, many enter the temple for the first time not knowing what will be required of them. Even after attending the temple, not much is discussed about the covenants and largely we are left on our own to learn them, gain understanding of them, and live them. Because so much information is presented in the endowment, some members haven't focused on these covenants enough to even be able to list them in their own minds outside of the temple.

For all of these reasons, we will discuss them here. Before doing so, please be assured that we will not be covering anything here that endowed members have covenanted not to disclose. I take my covenants seriously as a matter between the Lord and me. I am accountable to Him for how I keep them regardless of what others may do. Some have broken their temple covenants and published the entire endowment ceremony on the Internet. That fact does not relieve the rest of us of our obligations to keep sacred things sacred.

There are things the Lord has taught me that I do not and cannot share with others. Some things we must each learn and receive on our own directly from Him as we are prepared and ready. On the other hand, we each need some help along the way, especially when we are young and at the beginning of our temple journey. Sometimes our appropriate respect for the temple's sacred nature leads members to never say anything about it. We would rather err on the side of caution than say something inappropriate or, worse, violate a sacred obligation. This valid concern, however, can create other problems such as our children entering the temple unprepared for the experience. It also sometimes prevents discussions with other endowed members that could be helpful and enlightening.

So how do we know what we can discuss and what is off-limits? In the strictest sense, if you pay attention to the endowment instructions there are only a few certain things we covenant not to disclose. However, in a more general sense, we should use wisdom anytime we approach the sacred (see D&C 63:64). Our Savior seems to have always had His audience in mind as He taught. He often spoke in parables so that those who were unprepared for His teachings were not held accountable. This is also one reason the temple uses symbolism to teach us. Like the parables, the Lord has encoded by symbolism critical information in the endowment. The Spirit helps us decode that information as we are prepared. We would be wise to police any discussion about the temple in the same manner, with respect to the preparation of whomever we are speaking with. Some of the things I have written here and in *Understanding Your Endowment* are completely appropriate to discuss in a temple preparation class but I would not share them in a ward sacrament meeting. As in all other things, ultimately the Spirit must be our guide, keeping in mind our Savior's caution to not cast pearls before swine (see D&C 41:6).

THE ENDOWMENT COVENANTS

President David O. McKay gave an address to a group of young missionaries who were about to enter the temple for the first time to receive their own endowments. President McKay wanted them to better appreciate and understand their first temple experience. He stated:

> I have come over here this morning particularly because I have met so many young people who have been disappointed after they have gone through the House of the Lord. They have been honest in that disappointment. Some of them have shed tears as they have opened their hearts and expressed heart-felt sorrow that they did not see and hear and feel what they had hoped to see and hear and feel.
>
> I have analyzed those confessions as I have listened to them, and I have come to the conclusion that in nearly every case it was the person's fault. He or she has failed to comprehend the significance of the message that is given in the Temple. . . . These young people to whom I refer have become absorbed in what I am going to call the "mechanics" of the Temple, and while criticizing these they have failed to get the *spiritual* significance.[71]

In this same address, President McKay listed and previewed the temple covenants for these unendowed young men and women as follows:

1. The law of Elohim
2. The law of sacrifice
3. The law of the gospel
4. The law of chastity
5. The law of consecration

Let's consider each of these more fully to see what President McKay taught concerning them and also look at examples and teachings from the scriptures.

THE LAW OF ELOHIM

The first covenant we make is that of obedience. Some Church members are troubled by the way this covenant is worded in the endowment.[72] President McKay gave this explanation: "You will first be asked if you are willing to obey the law of Elohim; are you willing to take upon yourself the responsibility of making God the center of your lives? That is what it means."[73]

Notice it is not simply obedience, but rather obedience *to God*. Joseph Smith taught, "to get salvation we must not only do some things, but everything which God has commanded. Men may preach and practice everything except those things which God commands us to do, and will be damned at last. We may tithe mint and rue, and all manner of herbs, and still not obey . . . and teach others to *obey God in just what He tells us to do*."[74]

The scribes and Pharisees during the time of Christ were very obedient, taking the commandments to extremes, such as paying tithing on herbs and counting the number of steps they took on the Sabbath. Their leaders endlessly added guidelines, rules, and further restrictions beyond what God commanded. This resulted in the bitter irony that they eventually rejected and ultimately killed the very God who gave them the commandments in the first place. We might well ask: how did they get so far off track?

We tend to get into trouble when we add to or take away from what God commands. Sometimes that is very subtle. Notice that the commandment that God gave in the Garden of Eden was to not *eat* of the fruit of the tree of the knowledge of good and evil (see Genesis 2:17). Later, when Eve was approached by the serpent she added to this commandment by stating "God hath said, Ye shall not eat of it, *neither shall ye touch it*, lest ye die" (Genesis 3:3; emphasis added). Somehow the command of God to not eat was then extended by Eve to include not even touching it. This might have seemed a wise precaution; after all, if you don't touch it, you can't eat it. However, when Eve saw the serpent handling it without any apparent harm or death, it may have caused her to question God's original commandment. This error may have been reinforced when Eve touched the fruit and likewise received no harm. She then proceeded to eat of it, which action did violate the command and brought about the consequence.[75]

Joseph Smith testified of what he had learned from his experiences and mistakes: "I made this my rule: *When the Lord commands, do it*."[76] He further taught, "Happiness is the object and design of our existence; and will be the end thereof, if we pursue the path that leads to it; and this path is virtue, uprightness, faithfulness, holiness, and *keeping all the commandments of God*. But we cannot keep all the commandments without first knowing them, and we cannot expect to know all, or more than we now know unless we comply with or keep those we have already received."[77]

CHAPTER 9

The scriptures teach that we gain light and truth by our obedience and lose it through disobedience and because of false traditions and teachings that surround us (see D&C 93:28, 39). Christ testified that if we will do His will, we shall then know of the doctrine (see John 7:17). In other words, we learn through our obedience. After we do what God requires then we come to understand it in a way that those who don't will never comprehend. There is no way to become like Christ and His Father if we refuse to do what They say. We will not receive further commandments or direction from the Lord if we don't do what He has already asked of us. Lehi would never have reached the Promised Land if he had refused to leave Jerusalem. It requires faith for us to be obedient to the Lord's will because He rarely gives us the whole picture up front—it generally unfolds a step at a time.

As we move forward in our lives, we need personal direction and revelation from God. He knows our circumstances and the right path for us. Joseph continued,

> That which is wrong under one circumstance, may be, and often is, right under another. God said, 'Thou shalt not kill'; at another time He said, 'Thou shalt utterly destroy.' This is the principle on which the government of heaven is conducted—by revelation adapted to the circumstances in which the children of the kingdom are placed. Whatever God requires is right, no matter what it is, although we may not see the reason thereof till long after the events transpire.[78]

Timing is also critical in the Lord's plans. Another mistake that Adam and Eve made was in the timing of their transgression. Following the six periods of the Creation, Adam and Eve were to observe a Sabbath day of rest. Satan interrupted that rest as he convinced Adam and Eve to fall. What would have happened if they had waited for further instructions from the Lord? Would He, at some point following the Sabbath day, have given a command to partake? How often do we make mistakes in our lives because we don't trust the Lord's timing and prefer instead to take matters into our own hands?

As in all things, Christ defined obedience and left us a perfect example. When He appeared to the Nephites, He testified that He "came into the world to do the will of my Father because my Father sent me" (3 Nephi 27:13). Here is the scriptural definition of obedience to the law of Elohim. Christ didn't follow all of the social conventions of His day. In fact, He was rejected by the religious rulers of His day. He didn't obey all of the little laws and extra things they had added to the commandments, but instead He was perfectly obedient to His Father's will. We must strive to do the same: to do exactly what God commands, in the way He commands, and at the time He commands. The minute we depart from that and take things into our own hands, we are prone to stumble and fail.

Following King Benjamin's sermon at the temple (which was delivered to him by an angel), his people experienced a miraculous outpouring of the Spirit and then entered into a covenant equivalent to the law of Elohim. The scripture records their response: "And we are willing to enter into a covenant with our God to do his will, and to be obedient to his commandments in all things that he shall command us, all the remainder of our days, that we may not bring upon ourselves a never-ending torment, as has been spoken by the angel, that we may not drink out of the cup of the wrath of God" (Mosiah 5:5). As a result of this experience and this covenant, King Benjamin testified, "The covenant which ye have made is a righteous covenant. And now, because of the covenant which ye have made ye shall be called the children of Christ, his sons, and his daughters; for behold, this day he hath spiritually begotten you; for ye say that your hearts are changed through faith on his name; therefore, ye are born of him and have become his sons and his daughters" (Mosiah 5:6–7).

Like King Benjamin's people, you also covenant to do God's will in your life as part of your endowment.

THE LAW OF SACRIFICE

Obedience and sacrifice are closely related. It often requires sacrifice to obey the Lord's commands to us. President McKay continued his remarks on the endowment:

> Then you will be asked if you will obey the law of sacrifice? Nature's law demands us to do everything with self in view. The first law of mortal life—self-preservation, selfishness—would claim the most luscious fruit, the most tender meat, the softest down on which to lie.
>
> I am taking you back to the Garden of Eden, when man entered into mortality; the Tree of Life, and the Tree of Good and Evil, and everything which man desired was placed before him. And selfishness, the law of nature, would say, "I want the best; that is mine." But God said: "Take the firstlings of the flock and offer a sacrifice unto me."

That is the story. The best shall be given to God; the next you may have. God is the Center. . . .

You cannot develop character without obeying that law. Temptation is going to come to you in the Mission Field. You sacrifice your appetites, you sacrifice your passions for the glory of God and you will have the blessing of character and spirituality. That is a fundamental truth.[79]

Our Savior was a man of sacrifice. We often think of Gethsemane and Calvary, but His entire life was filled with daily sacrifices long before His ultimate and final Atonement. If our Savior's life was built upon the principle of sacrifice, then it should come as no great surprise that He requires the same of His disciples. The Law of Sacrifice in the temple testifies not only of our Lord but also points the way for us. The sacrifices that Christ requires of us are often small reflections of His own life, and they can help us become more like Him and better appreciate His ministry and Atonement.

Doing the right thing in our lives may also be hard. In the short term, the wrong choice may seem easier. It often requires sacrifice to chose the right, but in the long term it is always the best. In the end, the wrong choice will often be the harder one—not the easier. God always sees the long view even when we do not. We must trust Him enough to offer whatever sacrifices He asks of us.

The first sacrifice the gospel requires of us is that of a broken heart and a contrite spirit. It is to humble ourselves and accept Him. Lehi taught, "Behold, he offereth himself a sacrifice for sin, to answer the ends of the law, unto all *those who have a broken heart and a contrite spirit*; and unto none else can the ends of the law be answered" (2 Nephi 2:7; emphasis added). That can be a hard sacrifice to make.

We must develop sufficient faith to be saved. Both obedience and sacrifice are necessary for our faith to grow and increase. In the *Lectures on Faith*, Joseph Smith taught, "Let us here observe, that *a religion that does not require the sacrifice of all things, never has power sufficient to produce the faith necessary* unto life and salvation. . . . It was through this sacrifice, *and this only*, that God has ordained that men should enjoy eternal life."[80] We can only be saved once we possess this kind of mature faith. Faith grows through obedience and sacrifice. There is no other way to gain it. This explains one of the primary purposes behind these first two temple covenants.

Sacrifice of this kind and nature is rarely given in one fell swoop offering. Rather, it is given over much of a lifetime. It may not be easy, but it is possible. We sacrifice day by day to live the gospel, and it requires daily sacrifices to raise a family in righteousness. Missionaries begin to sacrifice early in their lives as they leave their homes to serve the Lord. In some ways, sacrifice may seem to be a wintry doctrine. But it is not something we should fear. It brings forth greater blessings than that which was offered up. Most missionaries can testify that what they gain by serving a mission far exceeds anything they give up in sacrifice for it.

Saving faith is mature faith. It is faith you have nurtured from a small seed to a mighty tree, which then produces fruit. Though larger sacrifices may eventually be asked, small incremental sacrifices are required all along the gospel path. They are necessary to help our faith grow and develop. Whatever the Lord may ask of you, give it or do it. Any sacrifice He requires is worth it and will be returned to you many times over. Trust Him.

The Lord has given us a way to know when we are on track:

> Verily I say unto you, all among them who know their hearts are honest, and are broken, and their spirits contrite, and are willing to observe their covenants by sacrifice—yea, every sacrifice which I, the Lord, shall command—they are accepted of me. For I, the Lord, will cause them to bring forth as a very fruitful tree which is planted in a goodly land, by a pure stream, that yieldeth much precious fruit. (D&C 97:8–9)

The Law of the Gospel

The next covenant we agree to live is the law of the gospel. President McKay explained, "In the presentation of the Law of the Gospel, 'the power of God unto salvation,' you will be told where to find these laws specifically, which you are expected to obey—in the Bible, the Book of Mormon, the Doctrine and Covenants, and the Pearl of Great Price. . . . God does not leave you without a guide. Too many of our young people throw them aside."[81]

If you search the scriptures for the phrase "law of the gospel," you will find it is not directly defined in them. In fact, in all of the standard works, this phrase appears only twice. So what exactly is it? We could say the law of the gospel is a broad brushstroke that encompasses all aspects of the gospel. It certainly begins with the doctrine of Christ that we discussed in part 1. But is there a way to better define or understand it? How could we boil it down to its essence?

I have given those questions a lot of thought, and in my opinion, this law specifically refers to the instructions the Savior gave in His Sermon on the Mount and again to the Nephites in the Sermon at the Temple in Bountiful. The principles He outlines there compose the *law of the gospel* that we should seek to live once we have accepted the doctrine of Christ. They are high standards. For example, He requires us to rid our lives of anger and contention (see 3 Nephi 11:29; 12:22); to be reconciled with our brethren and our enemies (see 3 Nephi 12:23–26); to rid our heart of all lust (see 3 Nephi 12:27–31); to return good for evil and to love our enemies and do good to them (see 3 Nephi 12:39–45); and to eventually become perfect even as our Father in heaven is (see 3 Nephi 12:48). Keeping these standards is no small challenge.

Other key parts of the law of the gospel are outlined in King Benjamin's talk in the book of Mosiah, which is also a temple sermon. He tells us we must also walk in the depths of humility, remembering the greatness and goodness of God and our own nothingness before Him (see Mosiah 4:11) and that we are required to minister to the poor and the needy in our lives (see Mosiah 4:16–27). This care for the poor is an important part of the law of the gospel as confirmed in the Doctrine and Covenants: "if any man shall take of the abundance which I have made, and impart not his portion, *according to the law of my gospel*, unto the poor and the needy, he shall, with the wicked, lift up his eyes in hell, being in torment" (D&C 104:18; emphasis added).

Our Savior taught our obligation to care for the poor with a story:

> There was a certain rich man, which was clothed in purple and fine linen, and fared sumptuously every day:
>
> And there was a certain beggar named Lazarus, which was laid at his gate, full of sores,
>
> And desiring to be fed with the crumbs which fell from the rich man's table: moreover the dogs came and licked his sores.
>
> And it came to pass, that the beggar died, and was carried by the angels into Abraham's bosom: the rich man also died, and was buried;
>
> And in hell he lift up his eyes, being in torments, and seeth Abraham afar off, and Lazarus in his bosom.

And he cried and said, Father Abraham, have mercy on me, and send Lazarus, that he may dip the tip of his finger in water, and cool my tongue; for I am tormented in this flame.

But Abraham said, Son, remember that thou in thy lifetime receivedst thy good things, and likewise Lazarus evil things: but now he is comforted and thou art tormented. (Luke 16:19–25)

This parable taught by the Savior has so many lessons worth pondering. Here we find an unnamed rich man and a named beggar. The rich man was probably well known and respected in mortality. Some would have looked up to him. Others possibly envied his position, his power, and his lifestyle. But it isn't until the next life that he realized he was sorely lacking.

Christ described the attitude of another rich man with the same problem in these words: "Because thou sayest, I am rich, and increased with goods, and have need of nothing; and knowest not that thou art wretched, and miserable, and poor, and blind, and naked" (Revelation 3:17). Viewed from an eternal perspective, things are often so different from how we usually see them here in mortality.

What did the rich man lack? Ironically, the very opportunity he needed—which would have changed him—lay at his feet day after day. Lazarus sat suffering at the rich man's gate as the world, and the rich man, ignored him and passed him by. Ministering to Lazarus's needs would have changed the rich man's heart and perhaps saved his soul.

King Benjamin likewise warned,

And also, ye yourselves will succor those that stand in need of your succor; ye will administer of your substance unto him that standeth in need; and ye will not suffer that the beggar putteth up his petition to you in vain, and turn him out to perish.

Perhaps thou shalt say: The man has brought upon himself his misery; therefore I will stay my hand, and will not give unto him of my food, nor impart unto him of my substance that he may not suffer, for his punishments are just—

But I say unto you, O man, *whosoever doeth this the same hath great cause to repent; and except he repenteth of that which he hath done he perisheth forever, and hath no interest in the kingdom of God.*

For behold, are we not all beggars? (Mosiah 4:16–19; emphasis added—and it ought to grab our attention—especially because Mormon saw our day and selected this sermon to include in his record for us.)

Each of us depends upon God for all that we have and for our salvation. In a very real sense, we are all beggars. The temple reminds us of this fact. One meaning of an outstretched hand is a symbol of the beggar. Once we are converted to Christ, He asks us to minister to others, especially to the least among us. One of the ways that His thoughts are different from ours and His ways higher than ours is in His regard for the least (see Isaiah 55:9). We are not to judge them, but to help them. That needs to be done in wisdom and in order. This giving of our substance is not required if we only have enough for ourselves to live from day-to-day. But even in those circumstances, we are forbidden from judging and our attitude is to be that we would help if we could (see Mosiah 4:25–26).

One day I was having lunch at a deli in downtown Salt Lake City. As I sat at the counter by the window enjoying my food, I noticed a man on the sidewalk outside. He was dressed in jeans, a T-shirt, and some work boots. Businessmen dressed in nice suits passed by on the sidewalk. I watched as he tried to stop many of them, obviously asking for a handout. People brushed by him without stopping to listen. Some didn't even seem to notice him. My curiosity at this situation led me to approach him after I finished eating. I learned that he had been unemployed for several months and that it had been a difficult time for his family. He was excited and relieved to have found work at a construction site and was trying to get there with public transportation. He had made it to downtown where he needed to transfer buses only to find that he was $1.35 short on the fare. He was desperately trying to find anyone who would help. I asked if he had eaten any lunch. He hadn't. Money was very tight for the family. It was an easy thing for me to give him the fare he needed and a few extra dollars so he could get a sandwich. He was extremely grateful.

This situation was a turning point in my life. Too many times I had been just like the businessmen passing by, oblivious to or unwilling to see another's need. Any of them could easily have spared the $1.35 in change and helped this brother. Yet none of them did. I do not say that to criticize or condemn any of them, as I have often done the same thing. And yet this situation caused me to examine my own behavior and to repent. Since then, I have had many sweet experiences where the Lord has been able to bless others through me.

I would invite you to be more aware of those you encounter who are in need. Before next fast Sunday, look around during the week and notice someone who is truly hungry or suffering in some way. Relieve some of their need. It may be a small thing to you, but it may mean a great deal to them. Then when you fast on Sunday, fast for that person. Do so with the attitude of sharing a little bit in their affliction and sufferings. You will find that your own heart is changed and your fast will have more meaning. As you do so, remember these words from our Savior: "Inasmuch as ye have done it unto one of the least of these my brethren, ye have done it unto me" (Matthew 25:40).

If we boil the law of the gospel down to its simplest form, in one word, it is *love*. Christ didn't say that the world would know us as His disciples by our doctrine, rules, white shirts, righteousness, power, standards, or anything else, but rather by our love (see John 13:35). He also taught powerfully that the first and greatest commandment is to love God with all of our heart, might, mind, and strength and then to love our neighbors as ourselves (see Matthew 22:36–40). When asked whom we are to consider our neighbors, He gave the parable of the good Samaritan (see Luke 10:29–37), reminding us once again that we are all God's children. We are to love everyone, including our enemies.

A friend of mine, Timothy, shared an experience that has meant a great deal to me, and I share it here for you to consider. One night, Tim had a dream in which he had died and stood before a judgment bar. Behind the bar sat a row of men. The man in the center asked him to report on what he had done with his life. Tim began to relate his life's achievements—career, schooling, family, house, cars, and so forth. While in the middle of doing so, some of the men behind the bar began to snicker, laugh, and even to mock him. Then the man in the center explained, "No, Tim. You were down there to learn to love others." At that point he woke up. This dream changed the course of his life. He now works daily to love everyone he encounters and strives to see Christ in them.

The temple and its ordinances and blessings reflect God's great love for His children on both sides of the veil. We could appropriately say that the temple is a house of love. We will feel God's love for us while we are there, and we should reflect that great love to those around us in our everyday lives. The law of the gospel is love. Love often requires sacrifice and must be coupled with righteousness or obedience to God's commands. In this way, these first three covenants are intricately tied together. Learn to love God and His children.

THE LAW OF CONSECRATION

The final covenant is the law of consecration. Before making this covenant in the endowment presentation, we also covenant to keep the law of chastity. Rather than discussing chastity here, we are moving on to consecration. In the next chapter, on temple marriage, we will address the topic of chastity.

President McKay introduced the law of consecration as follows:

> If in our souls we can accept these laws [the previous covenants of obedience, sacrifice, etc.], we are then ready, spiritually prepared, to enter the presence of God, provided we can obey the law of consecration, the next step.
>
> The law of consecration—"my time, my talents, and all that I possess, are placed upon the altar for the advancement of the kingdom of God." . . . And when you and I can stand at a certain place in the House of God and say conscientiously and truly, "I will consecrate my life, my time, my talents to the advancement of the Kingdom of God," we are then prepared through inspiration to enter into His presence. And that is what you do at the veil, symbolically, when the veil is drawn asunder and you enter into the Celestial Room.
>
> There, brethren and sisters, I have just briefly previewed the ordinances in the Temple of God. You will make covenants. There are certain things which belong to the Priesthood, signs and tokens that belong to the priesthood, which will emphasize the importance of the covenants you make.
>
> Finally, in conclusion I am going to say: Are you willing to keep your word? Will you keep your promise made this day? Are you a man, or a woman of honor? Will you keep your promise?[82]

As we grow older, we often begin to see that the things this world offers are fleeting and temporary, at best. The pleasure, popularity, riches, or success that people seek for and obtain here do not endure. Nephi foresaw that the great and spacious building, which was the pride and accomplishments of the world, would fall (see 1 Nephi 11:35–36). Think about those things that can truly last—our love for the Lord and others, our families, the service we perform, and the knowledge and experience we acquire. The law of consecration gets at our motives. Why do we do what we are doing? Consecration may be the opposite of competition. It is seeking to serve others rather than seeking to excel over them.

Nephi taught us how to live the law of consecration. You don't need others to join you. You don't need a formal community with an economic system where everyone owns everything together. What you do need is your own pure intent and to ask God to consecrate your labors for the welfare of your soul. You can chose to live the law of consecration today even if you are alone in your effort to do so. Nephi teaches us, "But behold, I say unto you that ye must pray always, and not faint; that ye must not perform any thing unto the Lord save in the first place ye shall pray unto the Father in the name of Christ, that he will consecrate thy performance unto thee, that thy performance may be for the welfare of thy soul" (2 Nephi 32:9).

You can consecrate yourself by giving yourself and your all to the Lord. You can consecrate yourself by loving and serving those around you recognizing, as King Benjamin taught, that when you serve them, you are serving our Lord (see Mosiah 2:17). You can consecrate yourself by serving diligently in your church calling. You can consecrate yourself by diligently serving as a home or visiting teacher. You can consecrate yourself by serving the poor and needy, the sick and afflicted. You can consecrate yourself by seeking to know the Lord's will for your life and then striving to do it.

Notice, too, how important prayer is in this process. Nephi says you must pray always and not faint. It is possible to serve the Lord through temporal as well as spiritual activities. How many of our daily activities should be performed unto Him? And how should we approach our relationship with the Lord daily? In the sacrament, we witness that we *always* remember Him, and keep His commandments, which He has given us, so that we might have His spirit to be with us (see Moroni 4:3). How closely connected should we be to our Savior and our Heavenly Father?

Of course you can't neglect your schooling, employment, friends, or health. You need to sleep, eat, and even set aside time for rest and recreation. But don't allow these things to crowd out the spiritual part of your life. Keep it a priority. Put the Lord first and then other things will take their proper place in your life. The scriptures warn us of the consequences of having our hearts set too much on the things of this world and the honors of men (see D&C 121:35).

Joseph Smith taught the Saints about the law of consecration with these words: "Now for a man to consecrate his property, wife and children, to the Lord, is nothing more nor less than to feed the hungry, clothe the naked, visit the widow and fatherless, the sick and afflicted, and do all he can to administer to their relief in their afflictions, and for him and his house to serve the Lord. In order to do this, he and all his house must be virtuous, and must shun the very appearance of evil."[83]

The Lord taught when He returns in glory in the last days, He will divide all people and separate them as the sheep from the goats. His sheep will be welcomed into His kingdom, but the goats will be told to depart. What is to be the criteria for the sifting? Christ will testify to His sheep that they fed Him when He was hungry, clothed Him when He was naked, visited Him when He was sick, and welcomed Him when He was a stranger. His sheep didn't realize they were doing that and asked Him, when did we do those things? (See Matthew 25:31–46.) Then Christ explains, "Verily I say unto you, Inasmuch as ye have done it unto one of the least of these my brethren, ye have done it unto me" (Matthew 25:40).

This parable is so powerful. Of all the things Christ could use to divide and judge people, this is what He tells us it will be. And look how concerned He is with even the least; this is one of the ways that His thoughts are higher than our thoughts and His ways higher than our ways (see Isaiah 55:9). Consecrate yourself to the Lord by serving the least around you. Be a friend to the friendless. Help the kid at school who is unpopular or struggling. Love and serve those around you. Christ will count these things as having been done to Him. He will not forget you or what you have done (see 1 Nephi 21:15). Consecrate yourself to Him by giving your whole soul as an offering unto Him (see Omni 1:26).

SCRIPTURAL EXAMPLES OF THE ENDOWMENT COVENANTS

As we wrap up our discussion of the temple covenants, consider what examples and teachings the scriptures contain of the endowment covenants. The scriptures and temple are closely tied together. As you study, look for temple themes. Watch for these covenants in the lives of the prophets. How did they live them in the challenges they faced and the circumstances of their daily lives? What things did the Lord require of them? What blessings did they ultimately obtain? This will help you to understand your own covenants better and how to apply them. Let's consider briefly a couple of examples.

Nephi recorded early in the Book of Mormon that his intent in writing was to persuade us to come unto Christ and be saved (see 1 Nephi 6:4). This raises a question: was Nephi saved? The answer to that question seems obvious, but if we accept that Nephi was saved and that he wants to help save us, then carefully looking at what he records can help us zero in on the things that are truly important to salvation. Nephi never had to get an Eagle Scout Award or complete the Personal Progress program, for example. Not that those things don't have value, but they aren't essential to our salvation. In Nephi's writings and in his example, we see illustrated the principles and the path that we must follow to be saved. As you read each of the stories he includes, ask yourself why Nephi chose to relate this particular incident from his life and how it relates to your own life.

Since the endowment covenants are critical to our salvation, we should expect to see evidence of them in Nephi's life. Can you see the principles of obedience, sacrifice, and consecration in Nephi's life? How were they manifested in his daily experiences? Do you also see how his relationship with the Lord grew over time? Nephi started with some doubts about his father's message (see 1 Nephi 2:16). It required the initial whisperings of the Spirit to help him believe and accept his father's message. He had to learn to follow and obey the whisperings of the Spirit, just like we do. It took time, and he had to grow. The Lord required sacrifices of him. Eventually all of these things culminated in the great endowment of knowledge that Nephi received from the Lord in his vision.

We see the same thing in the brother of Jared's account in Ether. If you look carefully, you can also find all of the elements of our own temple endowment in his experience. Once again, the result of the brother of Jared's humility, obedience, sacrifice, and consecration was to be redeemed and brought back into the Lord's presence and to be endowed with great knowledge.

Look for temple themes throughout the scriptures. The temple and the scriptures go hand in hand. One helps to explain and testify of the other. Together they provide us a standard against which we can judge truth from error and not be deceived.

HOMEWORK

1. Read President David O. McKay's full address on the temple.[84] Because it can be difficult to locate, a copy is available for download on my website at www.understandingyourendowment.com /q-a/david-o-mckays-temple-address/.
2. Study the book of Moses in the Pearl of Great Price. It contains great examples of the temple covenants in the early history of the

world, along with Satan's counterparts to each of these covenants. It is another great example of how the scriptures and the temple tie together. The table below summarizes this for you. (Jeffrey M. Bradshaw "The Five Celestial Laws" copyright 2014, www.temple themes.net, used by permission.)[85] Notice that the covenants in the left form the foundation of Zion, while the column on the right is the foundation of Babylon.

THE WAY OF LIFE	THE WAY OF DEATH
OBEDIENCE Moses 5:1–6	DEFIANCE Moses 5:13–14
SACRIFICE Moses 5:4–8, 20	PERVERSION OF SACRIFICE Moses 5:18–19, 21
THE GOSPEL Moses 5:58–59; 8:19	WORKS OF DARKNESS Moses 5:29–31, 47–57; 8:26
CHASTITY Moses 5:2–3; 6:5–23; 8:13	LICENTIOUSNESS Moses 5:13; 6:15; 8:14–21
CONSECRATION Moses 7:18	VIOLENCE AND CORRUPTION Moses 5:31–33, 50; 6:15; 8:28
ENDLESS LIFE Moses 7:23, 69; 8:27	UNTIMELY DEATH Moses 8:30

3. Another great example of the relation between the scriptures and the temple is found in M. Catherine Thomas's article, "The Brother of Jared at the Veil." I would also recommend you read it after you have been to the temple a few times. It is available in the book *Temples of the Ancient World*.[86]

Chapter 10

TEMPLE SEALINGS

*I*n addition to the endowment covenants, an additional covenant is formed between a man, a woman, and the Lord in the sealing ordinance of a husband and wife. This covenant is referred to in scripture as the new and everlasting covenant of marriage (see D&C 131:2). The five primary covenants of the endowment prepare us for this marriage covenant. They form the basis for the kind of loving bond that the Lord desires for His children. Build your marriage upon these covenants of obedience to God, sacrifice, chastity, and consecration. Doing so will bring you joy and a union that will endure. The new and everlasting covenant of marriage is the crowning covenant of the temple endowment.

At your temple sealing, you will be promised the same blessings of exaltation as were given to Adam and Eve, Abraham and Sarah, and many others. These blessings are made conditional at the time of your sealing. Their fulfillment will depend upon your subsequent faithfulness to all of your covenants. If you are faithful, then at some point the Lord will seal your union by the Holy Spirit of Promise. In essence, the Holy Spirit of Promise is the Lord's promise to you of eternal life and secures for you these blessings (see D&C 88:3–4).[87]

As with the other ordinances of the gospel, in the temple sealing ordinance, we again encounter both a physical and a spiritual component. We discussed this idea earlier as it applied to baptism and the sacrament, but the same is true of the temple marriage ordinance. The physical portion of this ordinance is performed as a couple kneels opposite one another at the temple altar and receives conditional promises. Following the sealing, they return to the world to work at living their covenants, becoming one, and starting a family. It is a period of growth and proving. The spiritual component of this ordinance can occur later as the Lord's final sealing of their union through the Holy Spirit of Promise. This occurs when He views the conditions have been met and permanently seals the union. Without both the physical and spiritual components, the ordinance and covenant is incomplete.

My wife and I were married in October of 1987 in the Salt Lake Temple. In the early years of our marriage, we tried to attend the temple weekly. After having children, that was difficult and our attendance became sporadic until they got older. About fourteen years ago, I decided to begin attending weekly once again. I wanted to do this in gratitude and appreciation for Christ, as a small thank you for all He has done for me. However, I soon discovered that this service blessed my own life in ways I did not anticipate. It changed me as a person and made me better. It blessed and strengthened our marriage, made it sweeter, and has been one of the greatest blessings of my life. Your personal circumstances may be different, but please do what you can to make the temple a regular part of your life. Doing so will bless you as well.

THE LAW OF CHASTITY

One of the endowment covenants is the law of chastity. We skipped it in the last chapter in order to cover it here within the context of dating and marriage. President McKay provided this explanation: "There will be presented to you the law of chastity, and you are going to hold up your right hand that you will obey it. What is that law of chastity which will be given to you? . . . It is the foundation of the happy, contented home. Divorce proceedings bear witness to the fatal result of the violation of that law. It is the chief contributing factor to the strength and perpetuity of the race. That is part of the philosophy of life to be presented in the House of God this day. And if you violate it, then you will bring sorrow upon your heads."[88]

Among the knowledge restored by Joseph Smith is the truth about our souls. "The spirit and the body are the soul of man" (D&C 88:15), and without both we cannot have a fulness of joy (see D&C 93:33–34). Joseph taught, "We came to this earth that *we might have a body and present it pure before God in the celestial kingdom.* The great principle of happiness consists in having a body."[89]

The challenge with having a body is that we currently live in a fallen, telestial world. When Adam and Eve fell, they fell physically, spiritually, emotionally, and mentally. We understand that we are subject to the Fall but may not appreciate the extent to which it affects us. Our bodies and minds aren't perfect. While in mortality, we are afflicted and live with many conditions over which we have absolutely no control. Eventually these restraints will be removed.

In addition, the scriptures teach that after the Fall, mankind became carnal, sensual, and devilish by nature (see Mosiah 16:3). The dictionary defines carnal as relating to physical—particularly sexual—needs and desires. Sensual is related to gratification of the physical senses and seeking pleasure. Our bodies are pretty well programmed to seek pleasure and avoid pain. There is much in this physical realm that is desirable and a great blessing to us, provided that we keep our desires, appetites, and passions within boundaries defined by the Lord. When we are outside those boundaries, we are offtrack and Satan has greater influence over us.

Elder Melvin J. Ballard taught,

> I should like to say to you, my brethren and sisters, that all the assaults that the enemy of our souls will make to capture us will be through the flesh, because it is made up of the unredeemed earth, and he has power over the elements of the earth. The approach he makes to us will be through the lusts, the appetites, the ambitions of the flesh. All the help that comes to us from the Lord to aid us in this struggle will come to us through the spirit that dwells within this mortal body. So these two mighty forces are operating upon us through these two channels. How is the battle going with you? . . . The greatest conflict that any man or woman will ever have . . . will be the battle that is had with self.[90]

Each of us has a dual nature—a physical side and a spiritual side. Our spirits and bodies are interconnected to a greater extent than we may realize. Our spirits are intended to master our bodies, not the other way around. When we commit physical sins, we often damage our spirits and lessen our sensitivity to spiritual communications. For example, the scriptures teach that he that commits adultery destroys his own soul (see Proverbs 6:32). The two sides of our nature are interlinked. The temple endowment provides a key to harmonizing the two sides of our soul. There we learn that our physical desires and appetites are to be kept within boundaries set by the Lord, which help ensure that our physical bodies are blessings.

Gratifying physical urges outside of the Lord's bounds turns something that should be a great blessing into something that can severely damage our spirits. When we allow ourselves to become addicted to such behaviors, then Satan has truly grasped us in the chains of hell. Deliverance from these chains is possible but not easy. Addictions can advance to a point of consuming all else in a person's life. How many have sacrificed family, friends, loved ones, careers, and more while seeking to feed their addictions? Marriages have been destroyed and innocent lives damaged simply by an unresolved addiction to pornography.

In addition to physical passions, we must watch emotional ones as well. We struggle with pride, anger, jealousy, fear, apathy, pessimism, and a host of negative emotions. These, too, must be controlled or eliminated from our lives. I love this quote from Sheri Dew: "Sin is just plain stupid. And the cost is off the charts. . . . Obedience, on the other hand, is brilliant and its fruits are endless—one of which is happiness. The only way I know to be happy is to live the gospel. It is not possible to sin enough to be happy. It is not possible to buy enough to be happy or to entertain or indulge yourself enough to be happy. Happiness and joy come only when you are living up to who you are."[91] Jacob sums it up in these words: "Remember, to be carnally-minded is death, and to be spiritually-minded is life eternal" (2 Nephi 9:39). In one sentence, Jacob captured the great battle of life.

One year, when my sons were both teenagers, I felt impressed to buy a milk cow. Thinking this would be a great way to teach them responsibility, I started looking in the classified ads for a milk cow. Believe it or not, it was kind of hard to find one. Still the feeling persisted, and I kept looking. About July of that year, I finally found a woman, Penny, who had a good milk cow she was selling. I called her to inquire more about it. She could tell pretty quickly that I didn't know what I was doing. Penny asked, "Have you ever milked a cow before?" Honestly, I hadn't. "Well before you decide to buy it, you better know what you're getting into," she said, inviting us up to her home that evening.

After work, I gathered my boys (and my curious oldest daughter) and drove up to Penny's house so we could see the whole milking process. We soon arrived at the farm and were greeted by Penny. While she patiently showed us how to milk a cow, her oldest son, Devin, emerged from the house. Devin had recently returned home from serving a mission in Spain. He struck up a conversation with my daughter, Jessica. Before we left that evening, Devin asked her for her phone number. In the weeks that followed, they texted each other and they talked on the phone several times.

Later that fall when school started back up at Brigham Young University, Devin called Jessica and asked her out on a date. That led to another and another and soon they were dating steadily and falling in love. Jess learned that as a young man, Devin had set a goal that the girl he would marry would be the first girl he ever kissed. He had kept this goal and had never kissed anyone while dating in high school or in college. Eventually, when Devin kissed Jessica for the first time, she knew how very much she meant to him. And it made her feel so special that he had waited and saved himself for her. They continued to date throughout that year and were married the following May. It was a beautiful day, one of the best of my life. Although, I still like to tease her that she is a one-cow wife, and I had to buy the cow!

Both Jessica and Devin had always wanted to marry in the temple. They wanted to go there worthily and without any regrets. During their engagement, they set some rules and boundaries for the physical side of their relationship to help them achieve these goals. I don't remember exactly what their rules were, but it was something like they would only kiss once a week and then for no longer than thirty seconds. They had fun with these rules—teasing and joking with each other about them during the week. Maybe that seems silly. It may not always have been easy, but they were clean and completely worthy on the day that they entered the temple to be sealed together. Even more important, I knew that Devin, who had already established such great habits and worthy goals as a young man, would be a good and faithful husband to my daughter during their marriage. Today, they have two beautiful children together and a wonderful relationship.

Now I recognize that their story represents the ideal and that not everyone's experience will match with theirs. But I hope that the lesson you will take from their experience is the importance of setting some boundaries and goals for yourself both before and after marriage.

We rarely get into serious trouble with the law of chastity overnight. It generally starts with small things that lead to larger problems. While serving as a stake president, a good friend of mine had to deal with some serious moral lapses. He once observed that sometimes it almost seemed like people woke up one morning and found themselves in New York City, far from their own home in California, and then wondered how they got there. Or in other words, how did I end up with this big sin in my life? And yet, they overlooked all of the little steps that led up to that point. They ignored the fact that first they had gotten into their car, driven to the airport, purchased a ticket to New York, and boarded the plane. There were a whole bunch of little steps that led up to the final outcome. Once they landed in New York, it was too late. We are all red-blooded humans and aren't as strong as we sometimes think. If we allow ourselves to get into the wrong situations, we fall. It is just human nature. The key to staying clean is to keep ourselves away from those kind of situations. It is the example that Joseph of Egypt set: he fled from the temptation. We need to set boundaries that keep us far away from ever boarding that plane. (No offense intended to New York City. It is just used as an example to illustrate a point.)

This is not just important during dating and courtship, but also after we are married. You should decide and set your own boundaries. My personal rule is very simple: it is to never be alone with a member of the opposite sex. That might seem excessive or silly to some, but if I personally keep that rule, then I will never find myself in a situation that could be compromising. The law of chastity is something that we all must come to terms with. You need to decide what personal boundaries will keep you safe and then keep them. Don't let yourself get into compromising situations.

Sometimes people want to know exactly where the line is. How far is too far? Our Savior gave an answer that may be difficult for us to live. He taught that we should eliminate lust from our lives (see 3 Nephi 12:28). Let the battle be fought there in your mind and in your heart. Keeping the law of chastity before and after marriage is a protection to you, because breaking that law brings deep regrets and unwanted consequences.

In many ways, the law of chastity is really about learning the difference between lust and real love and then choosing love. Even within marriage, spouses can approach one another to satisfy their own lusts or as an expression of love and service for one another. Choose real love. It grows and fills your soul.

When my daughters were in high school, boys frequently came over to our house to date them. I always wanted to meet the young man and, much to my daughters' embarrassment, have a chat with him. After visiting for a few minutes, I would invite the young man out to my garage where I kept a nice Harley-Davidson motorcycle. (This is a great reason to own a Harley for any of you dads out there who may need one.) It was a beautiful bike and most of these teenage boys were suitably impressed.

After the young man had oohed and aahed a little, I would then ask him a question: "What do you think I would say if you came over here and asked if you could borrow my Harley for the evening?" Most of them looked kind of shocked at this question and quickly responded that they would never ask that. So I had to push a little, "Yes. But what if you did. What do you think I would say?" Again they would hesitate, but then often say something like "Well, I would imagine you'd say no." "That's right!" I would respond, "Not only would the answer be no! It would be HECK NO!" I then continued, "Now, you haven't asked to borrow my bike but you are here to take out my daughter for the evening. She means a billion, trillion times more to me than this Harley ever will. Young man, are you starting to see how much trust I am placing in you this evening?" At this point, they were usually stammering or speechless. "Good. Now take care of her and have her home by 11:30."

The first few times this happened my daughters were mortified. But the young men treated them very well. Eventually, my daughters came to appreciate it. In their later teen years they would even occasionally bring a guy over and say something like "Dad, he needs the Harley talk." The young man usually had no idea what he was in for.

Young men and women, when you date, please recognize the trust that earthly and Heavenly Parents are placing in you. Never treat a son or daughter of God in a way that you would be ashamed of. Don't let your hormones take over. It doesn't matter what your friends are doing. You keep your standards. And don't go out with those that don't expect to be treated as sons and daughters of Heavenly Parents. Help one another keep the law of chastity.

Sometimes young women feel pressured to rush the physical side of a relationship. I counseled my daughters that if a young man really cared about them, he would take the physical side of a relationship slowly, not wanting to risk ruining the relationship. On the other hand, if he just wanted to get what he could and didn't care about a long-term relationship, he would go much faster and potentially further. Be wise in these things. If you lose a boyfriend because you say no, then he really wasn't worth having. If a guy cares about you, he will be respectful of you.

Perhaps in the Church, we do a better job of teaching the don'ts than teaching the dos of human sexuality to our youth. As a result, some enter marriage with unrealistic expectations or beliefs. We don't always teach of the wonderful blessings sex can bring in a loving, committed marital relationship. It is an important part of a husband and wife becoming one and can create an important, loving, and even sacred bond between them. To the Lord, our physical bodies, marriage, and human sexuality are all sacred. In the world, we find these things profaned in every possible way. In our own individual lives, we have a choice: Will we hold them sacred or will we join the world in profaning them? Recognize the difference between lust and real love. Lust never satisfies and will empty your soul. Real love, on the other hand, requires work, sacrifice, and effort but rewards you by expanding and filling your soul. There is a world of difference between the two. The Lord's law of chastity is designed to help you develop real love.

Keeping Our Covenants

As we conclude our discussion of the temple covenants, I hope you will keep a couple of concepts in mind as you strive to keep your own covenants. The scriptures make it very clear that the Lord will never, ever break a covenant He has made. He always keeps His covenants. The other important thing to keep in mind with respect to covenants is that the Lord is merciful unto us as we try to learn to live ours. Although we should try our very best, He recognizes that we don't keep them perfectly.

The opening of the dedicatory prayer of the Kirtland Temple reminds us of these two important truths. This prayer was given by revelation. It states, "Thanks be to thy name, O Lord God of Israel, *who keepest covenant and showest mercy* unto thy servants who walk uprightly before thee, with all their hearts" (D&C 109:1; emphasis added).

Because covenants are a very serious matter with the Lord, we should never enter into them lightly or without intent to fulfill them completely. God isn't trifling with us. The Savior put a parable out to the chief priests of His day: "A certain man had two sons; and he came to the first, and said, Son, go work to day in my vineyard. He answered and said, I will not: but afterward he repented, and went. And he came to the second, and said likewise. And he answered and said, I go, sir: and went not. Whether of them twain did the will of his father?" (Matthew 21:28–31). Don't be like the second son. Don't enter into covenants with the Lord without intending to keep them to the best of your ability. God will expect more from us as a result of our promises.

CHAPTER 10

The Psalms testify that in the final winding up days, "Our God shall come, and shall not keep silence: a fire shall devour before him. . . . He shall call to the heavens from above, and to the earth, that he may judge his people. Gather my saints together unto me; *those that have made a covenant with me by sacrifice*" (Psalm 50:3–5; emphasis added). Making a covenant *to sacrifice* is not the same thing as a covenant established *by sacrifice*. One is a promise to go and do. The other is a covenant by one who has gone and done. If we promise to go labor in the Lord's vineyard, then we need to go and give the promised labor. Our temple covenants and promises are conditional. They are an invitation for us to go and work in the vineyard. For them to eventually become permanent and sealed by the Holy Spirit of Promise, we must actually go and do the labor. Then we may receive from the Lord a covenant established by our sacrifice. Don't miss that point.

I want to focus on the hope found in the remainder of Christ's parable. Remember, He was speaking to the chief priests and the elders of the people. (These guys were supposed to be the leaders and examples. Others looked up to them for guidance.) And yet Christ warned them that they were like the second son who promised to go and yet did not. He testified, "Verily I say unto you, That the publicans and the harlots go into the kingdom of God before you. For John [the Baptist] came unto you in the way of righteousness, and ye believed him not: but the publicans and the harlots believed him: and ye, when ye had seen it, repented not afterward" (Matthew 21:31–32). We find here a very interesting contrast. On the one hand, we have the priests and elders who everyone sees as righteous, and on the other hand, publicans and prostitutes who were scorned and looked down upon as scum. Both groups are invited to repent and labor in God's kingdom. He doesn't discriminate. He truly is no respecter of persons and views them both as sons and daughters. But for both, the challenge was the same: they needed to repent and begin to truly work righteousness.

Here is the good news for us. It doesn't matter what the circumstances of your life have been in the past. Your past sins don't matter. Your life, like the publicans and harlots, may have been filled with mistakes. You may have grown up in a situation that was far, far from the Church's ideal. You may be very weak and in the world's eyes very insignificant. That doesn't matter. Your willingness to repent and come work with the Lord does matter. He calls to us all—each and every one of us. And He works with the weak and the simple to accomplish His purposes (see Alma 37:6; D&C 35:13).

You might feel like you can never measure up. Everyone feels that way at times. When you are willing to repent and let Christ work with you, then your heart is in the right place. All of us struggle, and even the very best of us are prone to weakness and failure. Peter, who was Christ's chief Apostle and one of His closest friends, denied Him three times on the evening of His trial. The Lord understands perfectly the difficulty and weakness of mortality. We are all here to learn and grow, and our covenants are given to help us become more like Him. He is loving and merciful as we work toward that end.

Remember, the temple ordinances are given to bring about our spiritual growth and maturity. That is a process and takes time. Growing from newborn babes in Christ to fully mature disciples is a lifelong endeavor. This shouldn't come as a surprise. We see this pattern of growth in any worthwhile pursuit in life.

I believe the very idea of learning and progressing is built into the wording of the covenants we make. We covenant to *observe* and *keep* the laws and requirements discussed earlier, rather than to simply *keep* such laws. To *observe* implies a period of watching, learning, and growing as we increase in our ability to *keep* our covenants. It is a process and takes time.

If you think about that, it only makes sense. You don't simply pick up a violin for the first time and play a beautiful melody. When the bow hits the strings in the hands of a beginner, the sound is grating and horrible. It takes hours of instruction and practice, followed by more instruction and still more practice to learn the violin. Mastering it requires many years. Only then can a beautiful symphony be performed. And the same is true with any worthwhile endeavor in life.

Is the gospel any different? Putting off the natural man, loving our neighbors, learning to hear and follow the Spirit, becoming more like Christ, and fully keeping our covenants requires instruction, diligent effort, and practice. It requires the very best we can give, but the process will still be punctuated with mistakes along the way. We will hit many sour notes as we learn to play the gospel melody. Ultimately, that doesn't matter. The point is to get our heart in the right place and then go to work. As we do so, Christ covers our imperfections while we learn, grow, and develop. We do not enter the temple for the first time as beginners in this process of learning to live the gospel. We should already be dedicated disciples. But we also shouldn't feel we need to be perfect before coming to the temple.

This statement by Elder Boyd K. Packer is comforting: "When you come to the temple and receive your endowment, and kneel at the altar and be sealed, you can live an ordinary life and be an ordinary soul—struggling against temptation, failing and repenting, and failing again and repenting, but *always determined to keep your covenants*. . . . Then the day will come when you will receive the benediction: 'Well done, thou good and faithful servant: thou hast been faithful over a few things, I will make thee ruler over many things; enter thou into the joy of thy lord.'"[92]

We need to give the Lord our best while at the same time relying completely upon His Atonement. Our obedience isn't what saves us—the Atonement does that. Trying to save ourselves is relying upon the arm of flesh, trusting in ourselves rather than putting our full trust in Christ. Nephi warns us against that. "Cursed is he that putteth his trust in man, or maketh flesh his arm" (2 Nephi 28:31). "Salvation was, and is, and is to come, in and through the atoning blood of Christ, the Lord Omnipotent" (Mosiah 3:18). Period. We are saved by the Atonement. Our obedience and our covenants are given to help us access the Atonement and grow to become more like our Savior. The more we appreciate just how much it cost our Savior to redeem us, the more we want to willingly follow Him.

We all need to repent. Despite our best efforts and intentions, everyone falls short. That doesn't mean that we shouldn't continually strive to improve. The Lord deserves the very best that we can give. We should strive to keep our covenants and to live up to the daunting standards He outlined in His Sermon on the Mount. It can be discouraging at times as we recognize how much we lack. At times, like Peter, we may find ourselves doing something that we swore never to do. All of us are weaker than we like to acknowledge, but this realization should bring humility into our lives.

As we move forward, we need to balance these two ideas. Recognize and remind yourself constantly that everything depends upon Christ, but then work at keeping your covenants as though everything depends upon you. He gave His very best. We should try to give Him the same, even when our very best may be like the widow's mite. He doesn't judge things as we do. Remember this promise: "Verily I say unto you, all . . . who know their hearts are honest, and are broken, and their spirits contrite, and are willing to observe their covenants by sacrifice—yea, every sacrifice which I, the Lord, shall command—they are accepted of me" (D&C 97:8).

Homework

1. What kind of marriage and family do you want to establish? How can the temple help you do so regardless of the type of home you grew up in? How do the five covenants of the endowment contribute to an eternal marriage?

2. What personal rules or safeguards can you put in your life to help you keep the law of chastity? Are you having difficulty with this law? And if so, do you need the help of a parent, trusted friend, or bishop?

3. The sealing rooms are an extension of the celestial room of the temple. This is more obvious in the older temples of the Church, but is still true in the newer ones. What does this location teach us about this ordinance? Does the sequence of the gospel ordinances also teach us something? How do they relate together? As the initiatory begins your endowment, is the sealing ordinance the conclusion of it? Are they tied together? Why or why not?

Chapter 11

THE TEMPLE REVEALS GOD'S LOVE

Some time ago, I had lunch with a good friend of mine who currently serves as a stake president. With a heavy heart, he shared with me some of the challenges and struggles facing his family. They had recently discovered that their youngest son had been abused by a trusted acquaintance while growing up. This son now suffers with some serious effects from this abuse. It impacts the entire family.

Another friend of mine has served faithfully with his wife in the Church throughout his life. The past sixteen years he has served as an ordinance worker in the temple. They taught their children the gospel by word and example, but despite all of this, today only four of their ten children remain active. Several have gone through difficult divorces. Others have left the Church. One has become an atheist and refuses to speak with his parents, and another has spent time in prison. Through it all, this couple continues to love and minister to each of them the best they can.

With the condition of the world that we live in today, there is scarcely a family that is not struggling in some way. The temple teaches us the ideal. It is good for us to recognize and to strive for those ideals. And yet you may find that your life or marriage doesn't match up or that there are situations or circumstances that are less than ideal in your own family. Those circumstances might be through no fault of your own or as a direct result of poor choices in your life. In addition to teaching the ideal, the temple is also meant to give and to testify of hope, even to those who feel their situations are less than perfect.

HOPE DURING THE STORMS

Another man has two daughters. He loves both of them with all of his heart and tries to be a good father. He and his wife served missions, married in the temple, and raised their children in the Church. They held family home evening faithfully each week, had daily prayer and scripture study, served diligently in their callings, and did all that they were asked to do. When his daughters were old enough, he took them weekly to the temple to do baptisms. The family was filled with friendship and genuine love. Their home was happy. They enjoyed working and playing together. Both daughters shared special memories and times with their father and were very close to him.

As time passed, the oldest daughter stayed on the gospel path. She met a wonderful, faithful young man and married in the temple. They have a beautiful young family and are very happy together. Her life has followed the path her parents hoped and dreamed that it would.

The younger daughter, however, made a U-turn in her life when she was about fourteen. She started hanging out with some kids who were drinking and making wrong choices, and she began making poor choices herself in an effort to fit in and be accepted by her peers. Her parents were concerned about this and tried everything they could think of to help her turn back around. But in spite of their efforts, she continued to withdraw from them and pursued a downward spiral with her life. Eventually she ended up addicted to drugs, her life completely out of control. Slowly, her world began to fill with pain and regret. Drugs provided temporary relief but then reinforced the cycle. Once a happy child, she became trapped in a miserable existence.

She frequently ran away from home and got in trouble with boys and with the law. She would return home for a time and then disappear again. Days passed without anyone knowing where she was. This situation caused her parents and her sister great pain. They tried everything to help this daughter, including professional counseling, rehab, and therapy. Her mother sat up with her several nights as her body went through withdrawals. For a time she would get better but would then relapse. Nothing helped in the long term, and the situation continued to worsen. Years passed.

The parents asked themselves over and over what they had done wrong. How could they have prevented this from happening? And how could they help their daughter? They prayed constantly for their daughter and kept her name in the temple continually. The father attended the temple weekly. This gave refuge, strength, and comfort to endure through these years of grief. Some weeks it was the only thing that saw him through to the next.

Eventually, the father came to realize that the question of what they had done wrong as parents was entirely the wrong question. He came to understand that this girl had been sent to their home not to prevent the situation from happening, but rather to provide her with a way back. Some lessons she would probably only be able to learn by making mistakes. It wasn't her parents' job to prevent this. And in reality, her parents really couldn't prevent it, but they could provide a home that was a safe haven for her to return to.

With this understanding, the man realized that all of his efforts to try to prevent her mistakes and to turn her around wouldn't work. The only thing he could really offer his daughter was love. And so he told her in the sincerity of his heart how very much he loved her and that he would always love her no matter what she chose. If she chose to be a drug addict that would have to be her choice, and he would love her anyway. He also told her that anytime she decided to come back home, she would always be welcomed. And he meant it. He stopped fighting with her and trying to manage her. He simply loved her the best that he knew how.

This changed some small but important things in their relationship. No longer was the daughter rebelling by her behavior because she was truly given the choice and the responsibility for her choices. For the first time, she began to really think about what she wanted for herself, although she soon moved out of her parent's home and in with her boyfriend. There she continued to party, use drugs, and live for the weekends.

Her parents could see this wasn't a good situation for her and tried to convince her to leave but she refused. Two more years passed. Eventually she broke up with her boyfriend and found she had no real friends in her life. Her addictions worsened until she looked like a walking skeleton. She ended up living with some people in a situation that was truly evil. Her parents once again tried to get her into rehab to sober her up but she refused to go. So her father took a week off work, packed a couple of bags and drove her to a hotel a few hours from their home. There they stayed together for a week. For the first day or two she sat like a caged tiger while the drugs worked out of her system. They spent the remainder of the week talking about her life and the choices she was making. She resolved to do better.

Shortly after returning home, however, she ran away again, returning to the drugs that had such a hold on her. Her family continued to fast and pray for her. They came to believe that these prayers on her behalf and God's mercy in answering them were the only things that kept her alive through this time. She no longer seemed to care whether she lived or not. Many of her friends had already overdosed and died. Week after week, her father sat in sacrament meeting pleading with the Lord that if she couldn't get better to take her home rather than let her life continue as it was for years to come. Her parents learned there really are things worse than death.

Eventually she met a new boyfriend and moved to a different city and a new life. Though not perfect, this situation was an improvement from where she had been. Her health seemed to stabilize. Though she continued using drugs, this stability was a step forward. Two more years passed.

One day this daughter came home to tell her parents that she was pregnant. She was very upset about it and had hid it for many months. Despite her mistakes, she did not want to harm her baby or have her baby suffer as a result of her choices. At the time, she was smoking a pack of cigarettes a day and using meth several times a week. The day she found out she was pregnant, she quit everything cold turkey and didn't go back. What she wouldn't do for herself, she found the strength to do for her baby.

Initially, her parents felt devastated by the news of her pregnancy. The night they learned of it, the man held his wife in his arms as she cried herself to sleep. Their daughter wasn't married. The relationship with her boyfriend wasn't ideal. Neither had a job or any means to support themselves. They were not ready to get married or to become parents.

That very night, however, a miracle occurred. At about five in the morning, the wife woke up to find the room filling with love and with light. She still felt very unhappy and dark and didn't want to be cheered up. However, the gentle joy persisted until she relented and opened up to it. Gradually the light and the joy increased until the room was completely filled with it. She felt some of the joy that existed on the other side with this pregnancy and this new little girl that was to come into their lives.

And then suddenly the girl, her soon-to-be granddaughter, was there by the side of the bed. She told the wife not to worry. She said, "Give my parents a chance. You can do it. I love you." With that she was gone. The next morning, the wife shared the experience and the insight with her husband. She felt immense love for her daughter and her daughter's boyfriend and knew that the Lord was in charge and loved them all unconditionally. She had felt and experienced some of that love through this experience and couldn't wait to tell them as well.

A few months later, the baby girl was born. When the man held her in his arms, he wondered who this little one truly was. He pondered on the service she had already given in her life just by being born into the circumstances she had chosen. Because of her, her mother and father are both living clean of drugs and have been sober for several years now. They are working to turn their lives around and to provide for their child. She is helping them to grow and to change when nothing else seemed to make a difference. The man and his wife hope to remain true to their granddaughter's wish to give her parents a chance. He hopes to help her in some small way to accomplish what she was sent down here to do. And he hopes one day to remind her of who she truly is.

Today, I can tell you that this entire experience has probably been the hardest trial of my life, but I wouldn't change it or trade it for anything. I am so grateful for both of my daughters and love them equally. In so many ways, my struggling daughter saved me. I grew up in the Church and always lived pretty faithfully, but my daughter taught me to truly love another with Christlike love. She taught me not to judge others but to look upon them with compassion. My daughter taught me how our Father in Heaven feels about each one of us and of His great love for us. She taught me about faith, hope, and charity. She taught me the things that I lacked. In many ways, she saved me, just as my new granddaughter is doing for her mother.

Some time later, my daughter and I had the opportunity of attending the open house for the Provo City Center temple. Afterward we went to lunch. My daughter remarked that because of her decisions in many ways her life was like the ashes of the burned-out building, but with some hard work and God's help, those ashes could be turned into a beautiful temple. She expressed her desire to one day be sealed as a family in the temple. Through her pain and suffering, my daughter has learned to have genuine compassion and love for others. Today, I'm very proud of her.

Down here in mortality, in the thick of the day-to-day battle, our perspective is so very limited. All of us, as God's children, truly are connected to a degree we scarcely realize. The temple helps elevate our view. It testifies of the equality and brotherhood/sisterhood of man. It also testifies of Christ's ability to heal and lift us. It provides us with hope.

Like these stories illustrate, many of us aren't in ideal situations. Some struggle in failed marriages, failed relationships, addictions, or even in the ashes of our own mistakes. Some suffer because of others' choices. Sometimes we can feel like broken souls. I believe that most, if not all, of these challenges are customized for our benefit and learning. We probably agreed to them before we came down here, when we had greater perspective. Down here we have lost sight of those things. It seems so hard sometimes, and it is easy to get discouraged, but sometimes our greatest mistakes are our greatest teachers. We need to be patient and to put our complete trust in the Lord.

Our perspective here is so limited. We have forgotten what went on before in our premortal life, the promises we made there, and the specific things that we were sent here to learn and who we promised to help. We need to be patient with the circumstances of our lives and to trust that many of the difficult situations we encounter are for our blessing and benefit. They may be providing us with the exact things we came down here to learn. It is also a good reminder to be charitable in our views toward others and to be patient and helpful to them in their individual journeys as well.

God is able to turn all of the circumstances of our lives to our blessing. Doubt not. Fear not. "Search diligently, pray always, and be believing, and all things shall work together for your good, if ye walk uprightly and remember the covenant wherewith ye have covenanted one with another" (D&C 90:24).

God's Love for All

One spring morning, as my wife was going about her day with a long list of things to do, she felt prompted to go to the temple. At first she argued with the prompting because she had so much that she needed to get done. But it persisted gently, so she changed her clothes and went to the temple. Once there she decided to do some initiatory ordinances, thinking that would be faster than going through an endowment session. Her mind was still focused on the many tasks that needed her attention. She soon discovered that there was an hour wait that morning for initiatory ordinances, but again felt that she needed to stay. As she sat waiting for her turn, another patron sat beside her and began to visit with her.

She told my wife about her life. She and her siblings had been raised in a home with an abusive father. After leaving home, as adults, they had not had much contact with him. Eventually their father grew old, became very

140

sick, and lay dying in the hospital. Most of his children still harbored such pain and hard feelings that they refused to go see him. This woman was the only one who would go, and she simply went to tell him that no one wanted him. As she approached his bed to deliver her message, her eyes were opened and she saw the Savior sitting at the foot of his bed. In response to her thought that no one wanted her dad, He simply said, "I want him." He said it with such love that the moment changed her life. When she realized that our Savior still wanted her dad in spite of all of his mistakes, sins, and weaknesses, she found it within her own heart to forgive him as well. She realized how precious each life is to our Father in Heaven.

Ultimately, the temple is about hope. The ordinances testify of God's love for us and His desire to bring us home to Him. The work we do there for the dead and for our ancestors is a beautiful reminder that Christ wants each of us. He cares, more than we can comprehend.

Speaking of these types of family challenges, Truman G. Madsen observed:

> [We] willingly chose to come into the world, likely in this time and circumstance. . . . And when [a young person says to his parents] in [his] deepest animosity . . . , "I didn't ask to be born," . . . the proper, prophetic answer [is], "Oh yes you did. You not only asked for it, you prepared for it, trained for it, were reserved for it." . . .
>
> This . . . is one of the profound meanings of that long, laborious allegory in the Book of Mormon, Jacob's allegory of the tame and wild olive [trees]. If you take a wild branch and graft it into a tame tree, if [the branch] is strong enough it will eventually corrupt and spoil the tree all the way to the roots. But if you take a tame branch and graft it into a wild tree, in due time, if [that branch] is strong enough, it will heal and regenerate to the very roots. You will then have been an instrument in the sanctification even of your forebears. . . .
>
> To be that kind of branch and achieve that kind of transformation backward and forward is the greatest achievement of this world. But to do it . . . one must be linked, bound to the Lord Jesus Christ.[93]

If you are in a difficult family situation, it may very well be that you are called to help save your family. The work we do in the temple is intended to bind and save and sanctify generations both before and after us. Don't give up on them.

Sometimes we focus so much on this brief mortal life that we lose sight of the fact that mortality is not just birth to death, but is actually the period from birth until the Resurrection.⁹⁴ Alma testified, "This life became a probationary state; a time to prepare to meet God; a time to prepare for that endless state which has been spoken of by us, *which is after the resurrection of the dead*" (Alma 12:24; emphasis added). The spirit world is an important part of our mortality. The temple is a wonderful reminder of this fact and testifies of the potential to repent and continue our progression even beyond the grave.

The circumstances into which we are born, the number of days allotted us in this fallen world, and the challenges we face are so different for each person. Like the sister who had given up on her dad, we may be tempted to judge and condemn another from our limited vantage point. God alone is capable of judging and weighing all of these things. We don't know fully what is in another's heart or if they might turn their life around like Paul or Alma the Younger. The temple ordinances are a wonderful testimony and reminder that *all* are important unto God and that *all* will be given an opportunity to receive what they are willing to receive from Him (see D&C 88:32).

The parable of the wedding feast testifies that both *bad* and *good* are invited to the feast (see Matthew 22:10). We are each invited to come and partake, regardless of the condition of our lives. We remain at the feast only by wearing a *wedding* garment, which we can only receive through Christ and His atoning sacrifice. It is the robe of His righteousness that must cover us (see 2 Nephi 4:33). Humility and the doctrine of Christ are keys to receiving His righteousness. The temple teaches and testifies of these things and aids us in the journey outlined by the doctrine of Christ.

It is my hope and earnest prayer that as you come to the temple, you will feel of His love for you personally and individually. Christ has promised: "I will manifest myself to my people in mercy in this house" (D&C 110:7). May you come to the temple to seek His Spirit, His love, His mercy, and His solace in your life. Come to His house to find Him.

Homework

1. Study Doctrine and Covenants 109. This section contains the dedicatory prayer of the Kirtland Temple. Joseph Smith testified that this prayer was given to him by revelation. That makes it the

CHAPTER 11

Lord's own prayer. Studying it yields insights into the Lord's purposes and intentions for His temples. What blessings does the Lord intend for you to receive from the temple?

Chapter 12
COMING UNTO CHRIST

The temple is about our journey home. Ironically, for each of us that journey begins in an unexpected place. We find it over and over again in the scriptures, for example, in the story of the prodigal son. After all the mistakes he made and after suffering for his choices, the scripture simply records that he reached a point where "he came to himself" (Luke 15:17). It's a beautiful phrase. It took hitting rock bottom, but this son finally realized he was perishing and resolved to return home.

For completely different reasons, Lehi reached a similar point in his well-known dream. We tend to focus on the later part of his vision and ignore the beginning. At the onset, Lehi reported that he followed a man in a white robe. Despite this guide, Lehi found himself in a "dark and dreary waste," where he traveled for many hours in darkness (see 1 Nephi 8:5–8). It wasn't until Lehi also "came to himself" recognizing that he was in a dark place and began to pray unto the Lord for mercy that he then saw a large and spacious field and the tree of life (see 1 Nephi 8:9–10).

King Benjamin's people began their journey home from the same place.

> And now it came to pass that when king Benjamin had made an end of speaking the words which had been delivered unto him by the angel of the Lord, that he cast his eyes round about on the multitude, and behold they had fallen to the earth, for the fear of the Lord had come upon them.
>
> And they viewed themselves in their own carnal state, even less than the dust of the earth. And they all cried aloud with one voice, saying: O

have mercy, and apply the atoning blood of Christ that we may receive forgiveness of our sins, and our hearts may be purified. (Mosiah 4:1–2)

We certainly wouldn't consider Lehi to be a bad person, and King Benjamin's people were also relatively righteous. He and other prophets had previously taught the word of God with power and authority and had established peace in the land (see Words of Mormon 1:17–18). On the other hand, it is easy to see the mistakes and sins the prodigal son had committed. In our minds, we would separate them and see them distinctly. And yet for each one the journey began exactly the same way—with recognizing that they were not sufficient on their own and that they needed help! Once their hearts were broken and contrite, they cried out for mercy from Him who is mighty to save (see 2 Nephi 31:19). And Christ heard and answered their pleas.

It doesn't matter how righteous and good and strong you think you are on the one hand, or how utterly wretched and weak you may feel on the other hand; until you come to recognize your total need for and dependence upon Christ and cry unto Him for mercy, you will not make any real progress in your journey home.

So now comes the real question: How is your relationship with your Savior? You can be fully living the *For the Strength of Youth* standards, or your mission rules, or the BYU Honor Code, and still be missing it! At its heart, religion is more than a set of standards for conduct. It is largely about our experience and relationship with God. It is about coming to know Him. It is about having our hearts and our very nature changed by Him and by His love and then reflecting that love to His children by serving and loving those around us. In fact, the scriptures testify that eternal life is to know God (see John 17:3).

So, once again, how is your relationship with the Lord? Are you coming to know Him? How often do you really speak with Him and pour out your heart to Him? When did you last hear His voice or receive His answer? Have you really recognized your weakness before Him and cried unto Him for mercy? Are you learning the language of the Spirit and how He communicates with you? Each of us is a unique individual, so that might be different for you than it is for me. It can also change for us over time as we mature spiritually. Our ability to hear His voice may start very small, but it can and should grow.

How well do you know our Lord? Do you know anything of His personality? Have you felt His joy in something you accomplished together? Have you ever let Him down and felt His disappointment? Or done something that amused Him? Has He ever chastened you?

What does He like about you? Have you ever asked Him that question? I did once, and His answer surprised me. Have you felt His love for you? Do you know what your standing is before Him? If not, have you asked Him? Joseph Smith was praying about that very thing four years after his first vision. Perhaps there is an example there for us as well.

What spiritual gift or gifts has He given you? How would He have you use them? Is your life on the path He would have you follow? If you can't answer these questions, then what are you doing each week in your church worship? What good is your religion if it isn't bringing you unto Christ in a very real and personal way?

Answers to these types of questions can only come by personal revelation. It is no wonder that Joseph Smith taught there is no salvation without revelation. Now, if you can't answer all of these questions or if they cause you to squirm a little, then take courage. Recognizing that something is missing is the first step toward receiving something greater.

Enos, in the Book of Mormon, was raised in a righteous home. His father was the prophet Jacob. Enos testified that his father taught him "in the nurture and admonition of the Lord" (see Enos 1:1). Today we would say he grew up in the gospel. And yet, Enos records that he reached a point in his life where his "soul hungered" and the words of his father concerning eternal life and the joy of the saints sank deep into his heart (see Enos 1:3–4). And so Enos knelt and cried unto God in mighty prayer for his own soul (see Enos 1:4). It is the same starting point. Enos didn't go to the trouble of recording his experience on the plates just so that you would know what happened to him. Rather his purpose is to invite you to go and do likewise.

You need to have your own experience with the Lord. Having our *souls hunger* is the first step. It doesn't matter if you've lived a very righteous life like Enos and Lehi, or if you've made very serious mistakes like the young prodigal—we all must come down in humility and rely upon the merits and mercy of our Savior. Humility is such an important part of what we came here to learn that we are all given weakness to help us have an opportunity to gain it (see Ether 12:27). For many of us it requires us to struggle with our weakness, sometimes for years, before we obtain the required humility. Weakness is a gift from God. If we don't gain humility from it, this gift may end up a curse rather than a blessing.

The temple testifies of God's willingness to receive us, heal us, make us clean, and welcome us back home as a son or daughter. In every case, whether the prodigal son, Lehi, Enos, King Benjamin's people, Alma the Younger, or the brother of Jared, the Lord heard and answered their cries. He will hear yours as well. Each of them had temple-like experiences in coming to know God.

Though my own relationship with God is the source of great joy, it is not always as close as I would like it to be. And usually, it is because I have withdrawn myself from Him, not Him from me. At other times, the Lord may step back to let us walk by faith and take some faltering steps on our own or to struggle forward without perfect guidance. This seems to be part of the required tutelage. Despite all of the blessings of the Lord in my life, I still get up every day and struggle to be better than I am. I can be filled with the Spirit on one day and then wake up the next to find that it is gone and I must work to regain it. Great spiritual experiences are often followed by periods where we are left to our own. Like Moses or Nephi, we return from the mount having conversed with the Lord to the daily squabble of life (see 1 Nephi 15:1–2).

The temple can serve as a spiritual retreat. It can give us our bearings and remind us of covenants, but then we go back to the world where we try to live and implement those things. I am very grateful for the things that the Lord has taught me and is continuing to teach me. He has gone to great trouble to personalize some of those lessons. He has taught me much but has also told me that I still have a lot to learn. He will do the same for you. Ask Him to teach you, then watch for His answers and be receptive to them when they come. He wants to talk with you.

He will draw near to you as you draw near to Him, but coming to know Him requires effort on our part (see D&C 88:63). Joseph Smith testified, "Let us here observe, that after any portion of the human family are made acquainted with the important fact that there is a God who has created and does uphold all things, the extent of their knowledge, respecting his character and glory, will depend upon their diligence and faithfulness in seeking after him, until like Enoch[,] the brother of Jared[,] and Moses, they shall obtain faith in God, and power with him to behold him face to face."[95] How well we know our Lord is largely up to us.

However long or difficult your journey may seem, it is worth it. All of this is eventually leading us to a fulness of joy. Eve testified that if it weren't for all of these things we would not have known the "joy of our redemption, and the eternal life which God giveth unto all the obedient" (Moses 5:11). Lehi tasted of the fruit of the tree of life and it "filled [his] soul with exceedingly great joy" (see 1 Nephi 8:12). Enos, too, found the joy of the saints and eternal life that his father had spoken of (see Enos 1:3, 27). No matter the challenges and obstacles in the way, Christ is our comforter. He gives "beauty for ashes, the oil of joy for mourning, the garment of praise for the spirit of heaviness" (Isaiah 61:3).

A HOUSE OF GOD

In 1832, the Lord commanded the saints in Kirtland to "establish a house, even a house of prayer, a house of fasting, a house of faith, a house of learning, a house of glory, a house of order, a house of God" (D&C 88:119). As we conclude our discussion of the temple, consider for a moment each element of the Lord's description of His house. Each of these items is related to and builds upon the others. In fact, we find a progression here in this list. This list not only describes the Lord's house but should describe our lives as well. If we are to become a holy temple (see 1 Corinthians 3:16), then our life must be a life filled with prayer, fasting, faith, learning, glory, order, and God.

A HOUSE OF PRAYER: Prayer is crucial to our spiritual journey (see 2 Nephi 32:8–9). We saw a great example of this in Lehi's dream. It wasn't until after he prayed for mercy that things changed and he made any real progress. Likewise, our own journey begins with and will be filled with prayer. It is critical in our relationship with the Lord. Prayer must include not only our petitions but also the revelations and answers we receive. One of the key differences between Nephi's life and Laman and Lemuel's lives was their approach to prayer (see 1 Nephi 15:8–9; 18:3).

A HOUSE OF FASTING: Fasting amplifies the power of our prayers. It should accompany our most sincere petitions (see Alma 6:6; Matthew 17:21). Fasting and prayer bring the Spirit into our lives and help prepare us to be able to minister to others (see Alma 17:3). Fasting can help to unite us (see 3 Nephi 27:1). Additionally, when the Lord describes His house as a house of fasting, He may be referring to more than simply abstaining from food. I think it also refers to disciplining all of the desires and appetites of our physical bodies. In the temple, we are admonished to keep them within the boundaries the Lord has established so that these things might bless our lives.

A HOUSE OF FAITH: Without faith it is impossible to please God (see Hebrews 11:6). He cannot bless us as He would like unless we have faith (see 2 Nephi 27:23). Prayer and fasting are crucial to gaining faith. Faith comes by hearing the word of God (see Romans 10:17). The word of God certainly must include the answers and revelations that you receive from Him in response to your prayers and fasting. Faith is further built through our obedience and sacrifice. This is the reason that we encounter these as the first two covenants of the temple. Faith is crucial to our salvation (see Ephesians 2:8).

A HOUSE OF LEARNING: The temple is intended to be a house of learning. We are to seek learning by study and by faith. Learning by faith involves receiving revelation and having the Lord teach us through His spirit and ultimately includes being taught by true messengers from heaven. Our prayers, fasting, and faith are first required. We also need to seek learning through study. We need to search, ponder, and really know the scriptures. Christ testified that they are close to His heart (see D&C 35:20). They should be close to ours as well. Almost all scripture is related to the temple and the temple to the scriptures.

A HOUSE OF GLORY: "The glory of God is intelligence, or, in other words, light and truth" (D&C 93:36). The temple is filled with God's glory. It is His great university, designed to lift and elevate us so that our lives might reflect some of His glory. The purpose of learning is to begin to understand God's glory. Our eyes are to be single to His glory so that our lives can be filled with light (see D&C 88:67).

A HOUSE OF ORDER: God's house is a house of order. The temple was meant to begin restoring the ancient order of things as existed at the beginning of the world. It was to help bring order to a world engulfed in chaos and disorder. Joseph Smith first introduced the endowment ceremony in the room over his red brick store in May of 1842 about two years prior to his death. Consider his description of the endowment. He stated that he spent the day in company with several others,

> Instructing them in the principles and *order of the Priesthood*, attending to washings, anointings, endowments and the *communication of keys* pertaining to the Aaronic Priesthood, and so on to the highest *order* of the Melchizedek Priesthood, setting forth the *order* pertaining

to the Ancient of Days, and all those plans and principles by which anyone is enabled to secure the fulness of those blessings which have been prepared for the Church of the First Born, and come up and abide in the presence of the Eloheim in the eternal worlds. In this council was instituted *the ancient order of things* for the first time in these last days.[96]

This definition of the endowment is instructive and certainly worth careful consideration.

A HOUSE OF GOD: Ultimately, the temple is to bring us unto God. It is about your relationship with Christ, and the temple can help you draw near unto Him. The endowment outlines the path. Your relationship with the Lord can grow from a very small and humble beginning and progress to the point that eventually you are able to stand in His presence. The endowment teaches about our individual fall and redemption. To be redeemed is to be brought back into His presence (see Ether 3:13). At its heart, religion is deeply personal and involves our own individual experiences with God. It is coming to know Him, allowing Him to change our hearts and becoming like Him. Eternal life is to know Him (see John 17:3).

The Temple's Testimony of Christ

Nearly everything about the temple testifies of Christ. The endowment shows the path He trod, a path that we must also follow. But the temple's testimony of Christ is much greater. "And behold, all things have their likeness, and all things are created and made to bear record of me, both things which are temporal, and things which are spiritual; things which are in the heavens above, and things which are on the earth, and things which are in the earth, and things which are under the earth, both above and beneath: all things bear record of me" (Moses 6:63).

The temple endowment contains one of the greatest testimonies of Christ that we find anywhere in the Restoration, though that testimony was not immediately apparent to me when I was first endowed. I couldn't see it any better than many of the ancient Israelites could see Christ in their ordinances. And, to be honest, it took me many years and some help before I could really see how our endowment testifies of Christ. Don't be discouraged if it is the same for you. Recognize that there is more to learn and keep pressing forward. Ask the Lord to teach you and to help you. Insights will come line upon line, one piece at a time.

Besides testifying of Christ, the endowment also outlines the path that we must take to return to Him and provides blessings to help along the way. This is perhaps more critical for you to understand. The most important parts of that path are plain and easy to grasp. Start with learning the covenants. Focus on really living them, and the rest will come in time.

Who Shall Ascend?

The endowment ceremony testifies that there is a veil through which we can communicate with Him and then ultimately find our way back into His presence so that He can complete our endowment. The temple endowment is to help us prepare for this event by teaching, blessing, and inviting us to receive more. It is an aid in the culmination and fulfillment of the doctrine of Christ. We symbolically make this journey back to Christ's presence in the temple ceremony, but we must also make it in reality. If we miss that point, we are no better off than the ancient Israelites who participated in the Day of Atonement and thought that they were cleansed and forgiven by killing a goat and a bull.

Consider some examples from the scriptures of those who actually made this journey and eventually received their full endowment from the Lord. The first chapter of the Pearl of Great Price contains a record of Moses's endowment. Nephi recorded his endowment in chapters 11–14 of his first book. The Brother of Jared's endowment is found in Ether 3. Joseph Smith and Sidney Rigdon recorded their endowment in section 76 of the Doctrine and Covenants. They concluded their testimony with this promise from the Lord:

> But great and marvelous are the works of the Lord, and the mysteries of his kingdom which he showed unto us, which surpass all understanding in glory, and in might, and in dominion;
>
> Which he commanded us we should not write while we were yet in the Spirit, and are not lawful for man to utter;
>
> Neither is man capable to make them known, for they are only to be seen and understood by the power of the Holy Spirit, which God bestows on those who love him, and purify themselves before him;
>
> To whom he grants this privilege of seeing and knowing for themselves. (D&C 76:114–17)

We are promised that our own endowment eventually can and should include this kind of knowledge for ourselves. None of us begin with this degree of knowledge, but it is where we can end up. Like climbing a mountain or a ladder, we must begin at the bottom and climb upward toward the top. Have faith, begin the journey, and don't become discouraged along the way.

How do we make the ascent? The scriptures ask the same question, "Who shall ascend into the hill of the Lord? or who shall stand in his holy place?" (Psalm 24:3) They also provide an answer: "he that hath clean hands, and a pure heart" (Psalm 24:4). Hands symbolize our works, and the heart symbolizes our desires. The Spirit is a sanctifier, a purifier of our desires (see 3 Nephi 27:20). Part of the blessing of attending the temple regularly is simply being in an environment where we can leave the world behind and be filled with the Spirit. Go to the temple as often as your circumstances will permit. Doing so will strengthen you as a person. Regular temple attendance will change you and become a great blessing in your life.

I close with His promise and invitation to each of us: "Draw near unto me and I will draw near unto you; seek me diligently and ye shall find me; ask, and ye shall receive; knock, and it shall be opened unto you" (D&C 88:63). May the temple bless and help you in that journey.

HOMEWORK

1. Reread the first section of this chapter taking time to ponder and answer the questions. How is your relationship with your Savior and Heavenly Father? What could you do to improve it?

2. One helpful way to improve your relationship with the Lord is by going to Him in prayer and asking for the next step in your life. What would He have you do? If you are sincere, He will answer that prayer. Go work on whatever it is that He asks of you. When you have completed it come back and report to Him in prayer once again. Repeat this process over and over. You will find that you will learn by the things He asks of you, and your ability to receive and recognize His answers and promptings will increase. Personal revelation will grow in your life and you will find yourself on a course leading you back to Him.

ENDNOTES

1. Ezra Taft Benson, "What I Hope You Will Teach Your Children about the Temple," *Ensign*, August 1985.
2. Ibid.
3. Boyd K. Packer, "The Holy Temple," *Ensign*, February 1995.
4. Joseph's wife, Emma, also spent much time as a youth studying the scriptures, and Joseph often asked her questions about the Old Testament and things he didn't understand.
5. Marcus M. Ladd, *The Temple Pattern: A Celebration of the Plan of Salvation* (Tafiat Publishing, 2015), 10. I recommend his book for a more thorough and detailed exploration of this idea as the plan of salvation relates to the temple and as found throughout the scriptures.
6. Not only is chiasmus found in the Old and New Testaments, but portions of the Book of Mormon are filled with it as well, providing another evidence of the Book of Mormon as an ancient text. For more information, see John W. Welch, "Chiasmus in the Book of Mormon" in *Book of Mormon Authorship: New Light on Ancient Origins*, ed. Noel B. Reynolds (Provo, UT: BYU Religious Studies Center, 1982), 33–52. The article is also available online at rsc.byu.edu/archived/book-mormon-authorship-new-light-ancient-origins/2-chiasmus-book-mormon.
7. The doctrine of Christ can also be found in the Old and New Testaments, but it is not spelled out as clearly. The Book of Mormon preserves the plainest teachings on this doctrine (see 2 Nephi 31 and 32; 3 Nephi 11; and 3 Nephi 27).
8. One of the few chapters that contains direct statements from the Father is 2 Nephi 31 (see verses 11, 15, and 20). This refutes a common myth among Latter-day Saints that the Father only speaks to mankind when introducing the Son.
9. Ezra Taft Benson, "The Book of Mormon—Keystone of Our Religion," *Ensign*, November 1986.

10. The *Lectures on Faith* were removed from the Doctrine and Covenants in 1921 by a Church committee.

11. *Lectures on Faith*, Lecture 3:3–5.

12. Sonya Colberg, "Oklahoma cancer patient trades her life so her baby could survive," *NewsOK*, October 16, 2011, www.newsok.com/article/3613629.

13. In addition, Lecture 4 lists several additional attributes of God that we must also come to understand. These include His knowledge of all things and that He has all power, justice, judgment, mercy, and truth. Rather than discussing these attributes here, I would encourage you to get a copy of the *Lectures on Faith* and study it carefully. It contains doctrines essential for your faith. It was meant to help you gain the faith necessary to lay hold upon eternal life.

14. See the introduction to the Book of Mormon.

15. *Teachings of the Prophet Joseph Smith*, comp. Joseph Fielding Smith (Salt Lake City: Deseret Book, 1977), 193. Hereafter cited as *TPJS*.

16. For an excellent book on this subject, see Colleen C. Harrison, *He Did Deliver Me From Bondage* (Pleasant Grove, UT: Windhaven Publishing, 2002).

17. Bruce C. Hafen, *The Broken Heart: Applying the Atonement to Life's Experiences* (Salt Lake City: Deseret Book, 2008).

18. Orson F. Whitney, *Improvement Era*, August 1927, 851, 861.

19. Wendy Ulrich, *The Temple Experience: Passage to Healing and Holiness* (Springville, UT: Cedar Fort, Inc., 2012), xiii.

20. *TPJS*, 151.

21. Boyd K. Packer, "The Candle of the Lord," *Ensign*, January 1983.

22. Ibid.

23. Jules Allred, "The Nature of God (Casting off the natural frame)," *My Journey—Learning to Rend the Veil*, learningtorendtheveil.wordpress.com/lessons/.

24. See *Wikipedia*, s.v. "Cliff Young (athlete)," last modified August 21, 2016, en.wikipedia .org/wiki/Cliff_Young_(athlete). Also "The Legend of Cliff Young: The 61 Year Old Farmer Who Won the World's Toughest Race," *Elite Feet*, accessed October 11, 2016, www.elitefeet.com/the-legend-of-cliff-young.

25. Ezra Taft Benson, *Teachings of Presidents of the Church: Ezra Taft Benson* (Salt Lake City: The Church of Jesus Christ of Latter-Day Saints, 2014), 36.

26. David O. McKay, "David O. McKay Temple Address" (Salt Lake Temple Annex, Utah, September 25, 1941). The manuscript can be found in BYU Library Collections. A copy of the full text is available on my website www.understandingyourendowment.com. ("David O. McKay's Temple Address," *Understanding Your Endowment*, July 16, 2015.) Hereafter cited as David O. McKay Temple Address.

27. Jules Allred, "The Nature of God (Casting off the natural frame)"; emphasis added.

28. An angel is simply a messenger. They can be from the eternal realms or can be a mortal servant of God sent with a message from Him. For example, Jacob taught his people the words God gave him (see Jacob 2:11). Under those conditions, Jacob was an angel, though he was still mortal. He delivered the words of Christ to the people by the power of the Holy Ghost (see 2 Nephi 32:2–3).

29. *TPJS*, 160.

30. *TPJS*, 150–51.

31. *TPJS*, 345.

32. Melvin J. Ballard, *Melvin J. Ballard, Crusader for Righteousness* (Salt Lake City: Bookcraft, 1966) 138–39.

33. Joseph Smith used this verse as an example of the errors that have crept into the Bible. He taught, "Look at Heb. 6:1 contradictions—'Therefore leaving the principles of the doctrine of Christ, let us go on unto perfection.' If a man leaves the principles of the doctrine of Christ, how can he be saved in the principles? This is contradiction. I don't believe it. I will render it as it should be—'Therefore not leaving the principles of the doctrine of Christ, let us go on unto perfection, not laying again the foundation of repentance from dead works, and of faith toward God, of the doctrine of baptisms, and of laying on of hands, and of resurrection of the dead, and of eternal judgment'" (*TPJS*, 328).

34. See David O. McKay Temple Address.

35. Ibid.

36. Ibid.

37. Truman G. Madsen, "House of Glory" (BYU multistake fireside address, March 5, 1972).

38. For a more detailed discussion of the endowment as a coronation ceremony, see Stephen D. Ricks and John J. Sroka, "King, Coronation, and Temple: Enthronement Ceremonies in History" in *Temples of the Ancient World*, Donald W. Parry ed. (Salt Lake City: Deseret Book and FARMS, 1994).

39. James E. Talmage, *The House of the Lord: A Study of Holy Sanctuaries Ancient and Modern* (Salt Lake City: The Church of Jesus Christ of Latter-day Saints, 1912).

40. Our discussion of the Day of Atonement is centered around Leviticus 16. For a more detailed exploration of this topic, see chapter 16 of Alfred Edersheim, *The Temple: Its Ministry and Services* (Peabody, MA: Hendrickson Publishers, 1995).

41. The scriptures sometimes refer to the Holy of Holies as the holy place within the veil.

42. Don't confuse the Old Testament role of high priest with the office of a high priest in the Church today.

43. John A. Widtsoe, "Temple Worship," *Utah Genealogical and Historical Magazine*, April 1921, 62.

44. John A. Widtsoe, comp., *Discourses of Brigham Young* (Salt Lake City: Deseret Book, 1941), 637.

45. Prior to 1990, the endowment's introduction did not include Brigham's statement as it does currently, but simply indicated that our endowment was to prepare us for exaltation in the celestial kingdom.

46. John A. Widtsoe, "Temple Worship," 62.

47. *TPJS*, 162.

48. Gordon B. Hinckley, "Of Missions, Temples, and Stewardship," *Ensign*, November 1995.

49. Silvia H. Allred, "Holy Temples, Sacred Covenants," *Ensign*, November 2008.

50. Boyd K. Packer, *The Holy Temple* (Salt Lake City: Bookcraft, 1980), 182, 265.

51. Gordon B. Hinckley, "Closing Remarks," *Ensign*, November 2004.

52. Ardeth G. Kapp, "Stand for Truth and Righteousness," *Ensign*, November 1988.

ENDNOTES

53. Ezra Taft Benson (Atlanta Georgia Temple Cornerstone Laying, June 1, 1983) quoted in Dean L. Larsen, "The Importance of the Temple for Living Members," *Ensign*, April 1993.

54. John A. Widtsoe, "Temple Worship," 63–64.

55. Ardeth G. Kapp, *The Joy of the Journey* (Salt Lake City: Deseret Book, 1992), 179.

56. See John W. Welch and J. Gregory Welch, *Charting the Book of Mormon* (Salt Lake City: FARMS, 1999), "Chart 92: A Comparison of Lehi's Dream and Nephi's Vision"; available online at www.byustudies.byu.edu/charts/7-92-comparison-lehis-dream-and-nephis-vision.

57. For a more detailed discussion of robes representing identity and being part of covenant ceremonies, see chapter 1 of *Understanding Your Endowment*.

58. For an interesting example of divine symmetry, see the YouTube video titled "Divine Symmetry in Nature: Number 9 De La Con Te 2015," found at www.youtube.com/watch?v=8qm6Rm9sT9c.

59. Hugh Nibley, *Temple and Cosmos: Beyond This Ignorant Present*, ed. Don E. Norton (Provo, UT: Deseret Book and FARMS, 1992), 15.

60. Admittedly, in addition to these seven, there is possibly an eighth division represented by the Holy of Holies. A discussion of this room and its purpose is beyond the scope of this introductory book. For that reason it is omitted from our list. However, it being an eighth division would fit symbolically with its purpose.

61. These notions were so deeply ingrained in ancient culture that out of respect and reverence for the threshold, a thief would not enter a house by the door (even if it were left open), but would only enter through a window or by digging in from behind. It was unthinkable to cross a threshold with evil intent toward the household. Something similar to this idea may have been behind Christ's observation that "He that entereth not by the door into the sheepfold, but climbeth up some other way, the same is a thief and a robber. But he that entereth in by the door is the shepherd of the sheep" (John 10:1–2).

62. See H. Clay Trumbull, *The Threshold Covenant: Or, The Beginning of Religious Rites* (New York: Charles Scribner's Sons, 1896), 10. In this manner, thresholds served as a primitive family altar. "The threshold, as the family altar on which the sacrificial blood of a covenant welcome is poured out, is counted sacred, and is not to be stepped upon, or passed over lightly, but it is to be crossed over reverently." To step over the blood on the doorsill was to accept the proffered covenant. To step upon it showed great contempt for those in the household.

63. Ibid., 60. In other cases, covenant words or other tokens were inscribed directly on the doorposts. These types of practices are found in ancient cultures from China and Japan to Persia, Egypt, Greece, Rome, and even in Central and South America. Throughout the world, various engravings, charms, shrines, or other markings were used to name and invoke the protection of the gods over the household and the members thereof. Even the children of Israel participated in some of these traditions and were commanded to write God's words upon their doorposts and gates (see Deuteronomy 6:4–9; 11:13–21).

64. Ibid., 203.

65. Ibid., 206. "Obviously the figure here employed is of a sovereign accompanied by his executioner, a familiar figure in the ancient East. When he comes to a house marked by

158

tokens of the welcoming covenant, the sovereign will covenant-cross that threshold, and enter the home as a guest, or as a member of the family; but where no such preparation has been made for him, his executioner will enter on his mission of judgment." Where no such welcome is offered, he must count the household as an enemy.

66. Ibid, 59.

67. See Dean Ravenscroft, "Lotus Flower Meaning and Symbolisms," accessed October 12, 2016, www.lotusflowermeaning.net.

68. See Alonzo L. Gaskill, *The Lost Language of Symbolism: An Essential Guide for Recognizing and Interpreting Symbols of the Gospel* (Salt Lake City: Deseret Book, 2012), 136.

69. Ibid, 91.

70. The instructor's manual states, "You may want to review the covenants just described by writing them on the chalkboard." See "Lesson 4: Receiving Temple Ordinances and Covenants" in *Endowed from on High: Temple Preparation Seminar Teacher's Manual* (2003), 16–20.

71. David O. McKay Temple Address.

72. The concern is generally with the current and past wording of the sisters' covenant of obedience, as some members see it diminishing the role of women. A little history may help provide some perspective. Joseph Smith first administered the endowment in May of 1842. For the next thirty-four years, it was then transmitted orally and not reduced to writing until 1877 when Brigham Young wanted to formalize the ceremony and eliminate variations then occurring in the presentation. He asked L. John Nuttall, Wilford Woodruff, and John D. T. McAllister to spearhead this effort. This occurred between January 14 and March 21 of 1877 and included revisions, discussions, and changes to the endowment ceremony before being standardized. Since that time, additional revisions have been made from time to time and will undoubtedly continue in the future. Wilford Woodruff seemed to believe that the underlying principles were more important than the particular wording. I agree with that feeling. My personal opinion is that we should focus on the temple's underlying principles (as taught by the Spirit) and be somewhat careful about how much weight we put on the specific wording. For a more detailed discussion of the relevant history, see Jennifer Ann Mackley, *Wilford Woodruff's Witness: The Development of Temple Doctrine* (Seattle, WA: High Desert Publishing, 2014). That said, there may also be a truth in the wording of this covenant that we shouldn't just cast away without further thought. It's not that women should be subservient to men. But there is some truth in the concept of submitting to and serving one another within a marriage covenant. That submission should be the man to the woman and the woman to the man—it goes both ways. The idea is inherent in a covenant relationship. I am bound to my wife in a different way from my relationship to any other person because of that covenant. Paul taught that husbands are to love their wives as Christ loved the church—even to the laying down of his life (see Ephesians 5:25). Ultimately, both spouses sacrifice for one another and for their children. This voluntary submission of ourselves to another is one means to truly live or change another and to bless them. Think of the example of Ammon and Lamoni in the Book of Mormon (see Alma 17–22). Of course this must be done prayerfully and carefully and doesn't require that we submit to abuse.

73. David O. McKay Temple Address.

74. *TPJS*, 332; emphasis added.

75. I recognize there are arguments about whether Eve was deceived or whether she partook of the fruit willingly and intentionally. I am not trying to take a position here. That discussion is not germane to my point, which is simply meant as an illustration of adding to or going beyond what God commands.

76. Joseph Smith Jr., *History of the Church* (Salt Lake City: Deseret Book, 1991), 2:170.

77. *TPJS*, 255–56; emphasis added.

78. *TPJS*, 256.

79. David O. McKay Temple Address.

80. *Lectures on Faith* 6:7; emphasis added.

81. David O. McKay Temple Address.

82. Ibid.

83. *TPJS*, 127.

84. David O. McKay Temple Address.

85. See Jeffrey M. Bradshaw, "The Five Celestial Laws," (2014), www.templethemes.net /publications/Meridian/100422-The%20Five%20Celestial%20Laws.pdf.

86. See M. Catherine Thomas, "The Brother of Jared at the Veil" in *Temples of the Ancient World*, ed. Donald W. Parry (Salt Lake City: Deseret Book and FARMS, 1994).

87. The Holy Spirit of Promise is discussed in greater detail in chapter 5 of *Understanding Your Endowment*.

88. David O. McKay Temple Address.

89. *TPJS*, 181; emphasis added.

90. Address delivered in the Salt Lake Tabernacle on May 5, 1928. See Melvin J. Ballard, "Struggle for the Soul," *New Era*, March 1984.

91. Sheri L. Dew, "You Were Born to Lead, You Were Born for Glory" (Brigham Young University speech, December 9, 2003); speeches.byu.edu.

92. Boyd K. Packer, *Let Not Your Heart Be Troubled* (Salt Lake City: Bookcraft, 1991), 257; emphasis added.

93. As quoted in Jeffrey M. Bradshaw, *Temple Themes in the Oath and Covenant of the Priesthood* (West Valley City, UT: Eborn Publishing, 2012), 44.

94. President Boyd K. Packer taught; "The plan of redemption, with its three divisions, might be likened to a grand three-act play. Act I is entitled 'Premortal Life.' The scriptures describe it as our First Estate. Act II, from birth to the time of resurrection, the 'Second Estate.' And Act III, 'Life After Death or Eternal Life.'" (Boyd K. Packer, "The Play and the Plan," [Church Educational System fireside, May 7, 1995], 1; emphasis added.) This idea of mortality (or our probationary state) being the period between birth and the resurrection is also found in Alma 12:24.

95. *Lectures on Faith*, 2:55.

96. Joseph Smith Jr., *History of the Church* (Salt Lake City: Deseret Book, 1991), 5:1–2; emphasis added.

ABOUT
THE AUTHOR

*C*ory B. Jensen was born and raised in Utah and grew up in the shadow of the Logan Temple. He developed a love for the temple early in life and has been an avid student ever since. He graduated with honors from Brigham Young University with a master of business administration. A lifelong devoted member of The Church of Jesus Christ of Latter-day Saints, he served a mission in Rome, Italy, and is looking forward to the completion of the temple there.

He and his wife, Traci, are the parents of four children and served together as ordinance workers in the Mount Timpanogos Utah Temple. That service has greatly blessed their lives and the lives of their family.

He hopes the message of this book will bless your life, enrich your personal temple experience, and help you prepare for and better understand your own endowment.

SCAN to visit

www.understandingyourendowment.com